THE COMPLETE BOOK OF
BONES

AN INTRODUCTION TO SKELETONS

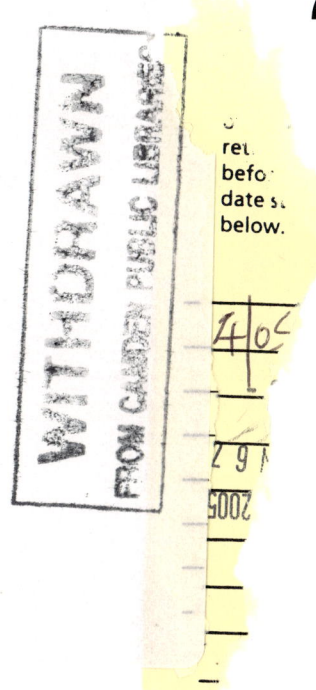

Claire Llewellyn

Hodder
Wayland

an imprint of Hodder Children's Books

Words in **bold** are explained in the glossary.

First published in Great Britain in 1998
by Macdonald Young Books,
an imprint of Wayland Publishers Ltd.

This paperback edition published in 2001
by Hodder Wayland, an imprint of
Hodder Children's Books

© Hodder Wayland 1998

Hodder Children's Books
A division of Hodder Headline Limited
338 Euston Road, London NW1 3BH

Text © Claire Llewellyn, 1998

Illustrations © Peter Geissler (Specs Art)
and Bruce Hogarth (David Lewis Agency), 1998

All rights reserved

A CIP catalogue record for this book is available from
the British Library

Cover design: Chris Leishman and Mike Rose
Insides design: Casebourne Rose Design Associates
Editors: Fiona Corbridge and Penny McDowell
Consultant: Dr Richard Walker

Special thanks to:
Jeremy Adams at the Booth Museum, Brighton.

Printed and bound in Portugal by Edições ASA

ISBN 0 7502 3678 7

Contents

A framework of clues 4
What is a skeleton? 6
On the move 8
Living in a skeleton 10
Underwater armour 12
Inside a shell 14
Skeletons in the sea 16
Fish bones 18
Rugged reptiles 20
Flying skeletons 22
Monster and mini mammals 24
The human skeleton - skull to hips 26
The human skeleton - hips to feet 28
The human skull 30
Looking at bones 32
Bones for life 34
Animal skulls 36
Arms, flippers and wings 38
Legs, feet and hooves 40
Bones from the past 42
Scary bones 44
Quiz 46
Glossary 47
Acknowledgements 47
Index 48

A Framework of Clues

A skeleton is the hard framework that holds up an animal's body and protects all the soft parts inside. Animals come in all shapes and sizes, and so do their skeletons. A mighty elephant needs heavyweight bones, while those of a mouse are tiny and light.

Whose skeleton?

Scientists have learned to look carefully at skeletons, and ask questions about what they see. A skeleton tells us a lot more about an animal than just its size, shape or weight. The bones give important clues to many different aspects of its life. The leg bones show how it moved, and whether it could swim, jump or fly. The jaws and teeth reveal what kind of food it ate – whether it hunted other animals, or grazed peacefully on leaves and grass. The skull provides information about how the animal interpreted the world around it. It tells us whether it had good eyesight, sharp hearing or a keen sense of smell. This book introduces the skeletons of many kinds of animal, and explains how they move and why they look the way they do. And it shows how, over millions of years, an animal's **habitat** and way of life have shaped its skeleton today.

Above A frog skeleton has long legs and toes. The skull has large eye sockets. The papery bags are air sacs. The frog uses the top pair of air sacs to croak and the bottom pair to breathe.

Right Frogs jump high with their springy back legs. They have long toes which, covered by skin, make useful flippers in the water. Their sharp eyes help them to catch plenty of juicy flies and other small creatures.

THE BIG BOOK OF BONES 5

Above This skeleton is long and narrow, with a strong, pointed skull and short legs. The front legs are thicker and heavier than the back. It's the skeleton of a mole.

Right Moles use their powerful front legs and paws like shovels to dig out underground tunnels. Their pointed snout pushes forwards as they burrow through the soil.

Right This skeleton is very light. It belonged to an animal with a supple spine, long tail, and sharp claws. In the skull, there are four enormous teeth. This skeleton belonged to a red squirrel.

Above Squirrels use their bushy tail to balance as they leap through the trees, gripping on tightly with their claws. Their long teeth are designed to crack open nuts so they can gnaw the kernels inside.

What is a Skeleton?

A skeleton is an important part of a body. It forms a strong framework, supporting the body's weight, and giving it its own particular shape. The skeleton also protects the soft, essential organs such as the brain, lungs, and heart, on which we depend for life. Lastly, the skeleton helps us to move. Our bones work with **muscles** to move our bodies, so that, for example, we can walk to a shelf, pick up a book and turn a page.

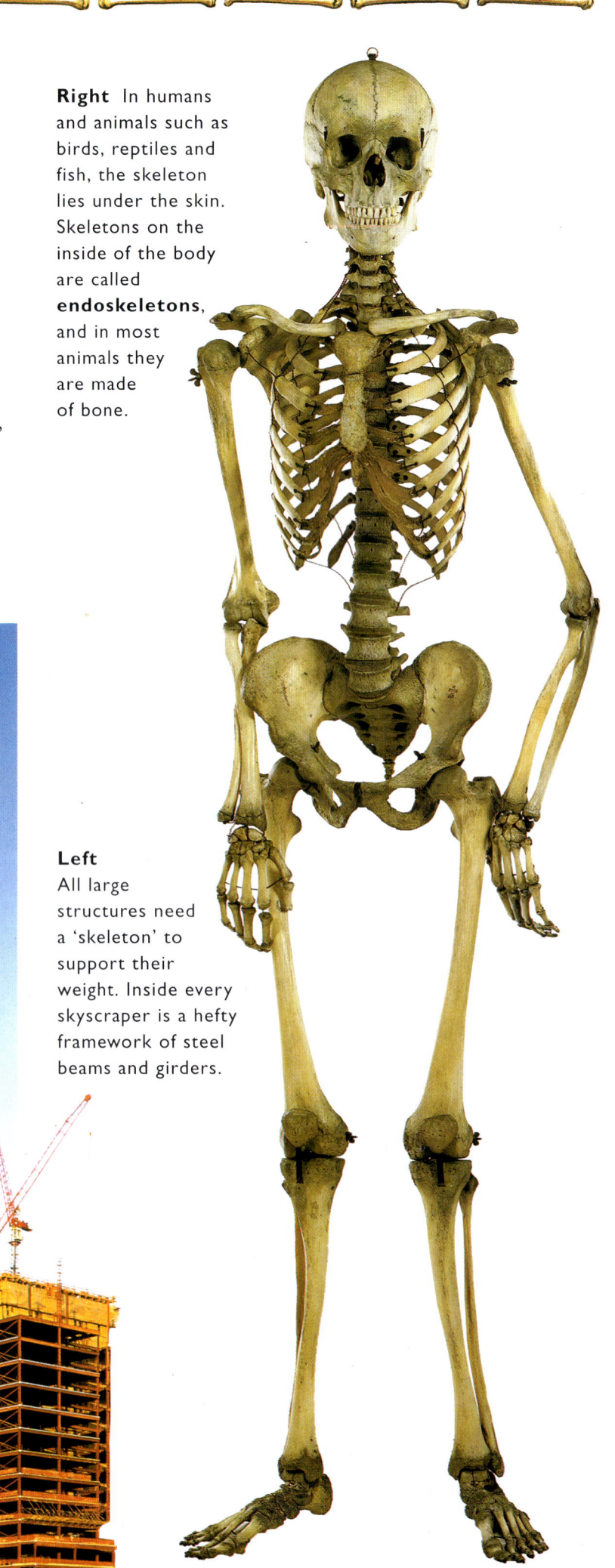

Right In humans and animals such as birds, reptiles and fish, the skeleton lies under the skin. Skeletons on the inside of the body are called **endoskeletons**, and in most animals they are made of bone.

Left All large structures need a 'skeleton' to support their weight. Inside every skyscraper is a hefty framework of steel beams and girders.

THE BIG BOOK OF BONES 7

Right Without a skeleton, your body would be floppy, shapeless and still – rather like a T-shirt thrown on the floor.

Bag of bones

It is an amazing thought that everyone you meet is a walking collection of bones. Adults have roughly 200 bones inside them. Our bones vary greatly in their size and shape. Some are long and straight with knobbly ends, others are curved, and a few are small and round like pebbles. This varied collection fits together to form the skeleton, a sturdy yet flexible structure. Each part of the skeleton has its own special task. For example, the skull is a strongbox designed to protect the brain; the bones in the arm and hand form a piece of machinery that can move with both power and skill.

Right A helmet-like skull to protect the brain, a cage to protect the heart, strong legs to stand on, fingers to touch and grasp – every part of the skeleton is designed to do its own particular job.

BONE UP!

- Your skeleton makes up less than one-fifth of your total weight.
- Many people are as broad as they're long. Ask someone to measure your arm span and height, and see if they measure the same.
- Most of us have twelve pairs of ribs. But a few people have one more or one less.
- The smallest, lightest bone in the body lies deep inside your ear. It is smaller than a grain of rice.
- The tallest man ever was an American called Robert Wadlow, who measured 2.7 m. That's roughly as high as most ceilings.
- There's enough room inside your hollow skull for a litre and a half of liquid: that's the drink inside over four cans of cola.

ON THE MOVE

Every move we make depends on our bones and muscles working together. When we want to move, our brain sends a signal to our muscles, telling them to **contract**. When muscles contract, they pull on tough cords called **tendons**, which then move our bones. Without bones, our muscles would have nothing to pull on; without muscles, our bones couldn't move.

Left and below Hundreds of muscles and dozens of bones help us to balance and stretch. Exercising our muscles keeps them strong and supple. Dancers warm up their muscles before every performance by doing some gentle exercise.

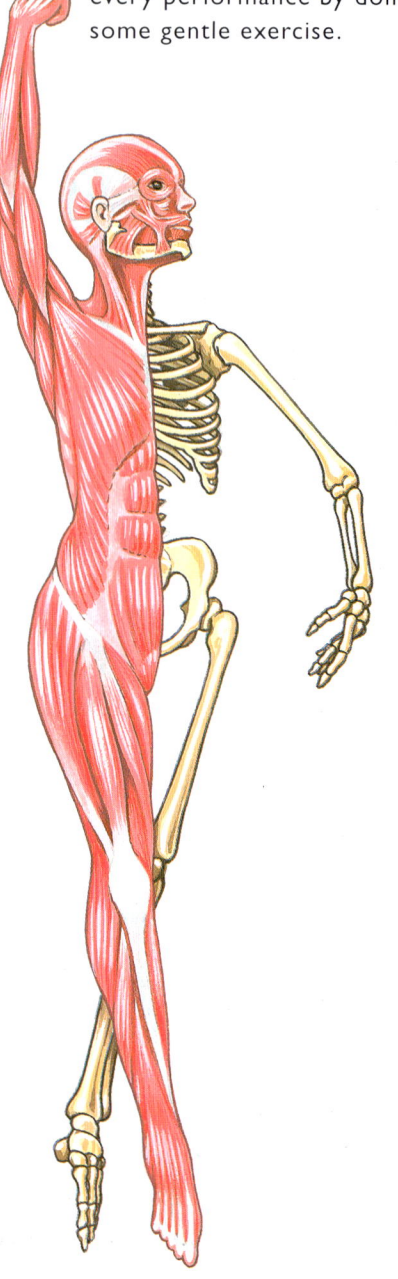

Joints

A skeleton can only move at places, called joints, where two bones meet. There are two main kinds of joint.

Hip joint

Elbow joint

A **ball-and-socket** joint swivels round in almost any direction. It is found in your shoulders and hips.

A **hinge** joint allows a bone to bend or straighten. Hinge joints are found in your fingers, elbows and knees.

In working order

Our joints move countless times every day. Without some form of protection, the bones would slip out of place or grind together and lose their shape. To avoid this, bones are bound at the joints by straps called **ligaments**, which keep the bones firmly in place. The whole joint is coated in an oily liquid, which helps it to move smoothly and easily, over and over again.

Animals afoot

An animal's skeleton is closely linked to the way that it moves. The bones' size, length, weight, and the way they are put together determine whether the animal wriggles, jumps or runs like the wind. A fast-moving **predator**, such as the cheetah, has long, slim leg bones and a very flexible backbone. When powerful muscles pull on these bones, the cheetah's supple backbone flexes, and its legs stretch out in an incredible stride. This is the secret of its record-breaking speed.

Crusty creatures

Some animals don't have bones. Insects and many other small creatures have a hard outer casing called an **exoskeleton**, made up of small rigid plates. These plates meet at joints, where the exoskeleton is thinner and much more flexible. It yields just enough for muscles under the joints to pull on the plates, which in turn moves the animals' limbs.

Above Every bit of a spider is covered by a hard exoskeleton, even its eyes. But the creature is able to move because its legs are made in many segments, hinged together, and joined by muscles.

BONE UP!

- The more you exercise your muscles, the stronger your bones become.
- Humans have about 650 muscles – around three for every bone in the body.
- It's easier to move the bits of the body where joints lie close together. The many joints in your backbone allow you to bend almost double.
- Not all joints can move. Most of the bones in your skull have fixed joints that can't move at all.
- The muscles in your body weigh more than the bones.

LIVING IN A SKELETON

Our skeleton is a framework of bones that lies hidden under the skin, but many other animals have a very different kind of skeleton. Most animals on Earth are **invertebrates**. This means they have no backbone, and no bony skeleton. Instead, many of them have a hard, crusty casing outside their body, rather like a suit of armour. This is called an exoskeleton ('exo' comes from a Greek word, meaning 'outside').

Armourplating

The exoskeleton covers the whole body. It is made mainly of a tough material called **chitin**, which feels a bit like our fingernails. Some parts of the body, such as the head, back and legs, are covered by thick, horny plates; in other places, such as wings and eyes, the exoskeleton is so fine that it is transparent. The exoskeleton supports and protects an animal's body, and helps different parts of it to move. Sometimes it provides the creature with extra tools. A scorpion's exoskeleton supplies it with a strong pair of pincers, razor-edged jaws, and a long, sharp sting on its tail. Some fierce beetles have pointed spikes and horns.

Below A scorpion's exoskeleton is both a protective armour and a weapons system!

THE BIG BOOK OF BONES 11

Above In the Middle Ages, knights were sometimes so weighed down by heavy armour that they could hardly move! They had to be winched on to their horses.

Animals with exoskeletons are usually small. If they grew any larger, their exoskeleton (like the knights' armour) would be much too heavy to move.

Bursting skeletons

Exoskeletons have many advantages, but they also have one big drawback: animals have to shed them in order to grow. As the animal grows, its exoskeleton becomes too tight, and bursts at the seams. Underneath it has a soft, new exoskeleton, which hardens on contact with the air.

Above A grasshopper wriggles out of its exoskeleton, leaving the old, empty case behind.

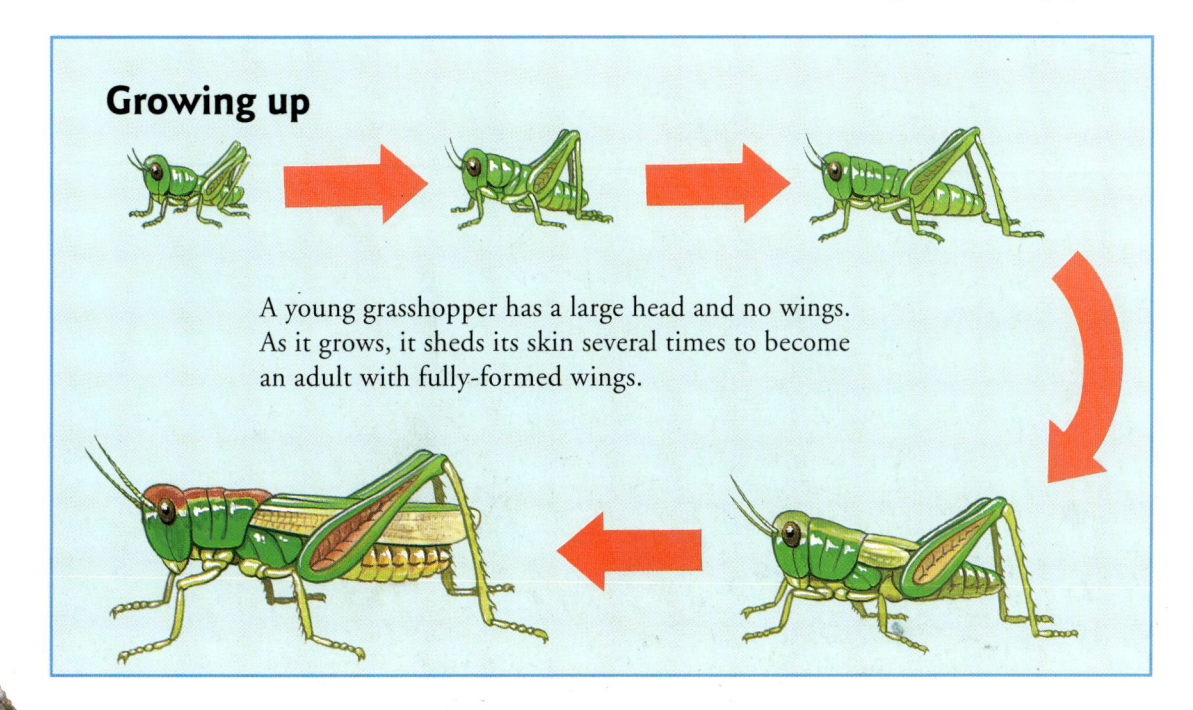

Growing up

A young grasshopper has a large head and no wings. As it grows, it sheds its skin several times to become an adult with fully-formed wings.

BONE UP!

- Nine out of ten of all types of animal have an exoskeleton.
- A woodlouse depends on its exoskeleton to protect it from enemies. When it is threatened, it rolls up tightly in a little armoured ball.
- After shedding its skin, a spider is soft and unprotected, and needs to hide from its enemies.

Underwater Armour

Prawns, lobsters, crabs and shrimps are just some of the invertebrates that live in the sea. They belong to an animal group called **crustaceans**, which have jointed bodies covered by a hard, crusty shell (the exoskeleton). Many of these sea creatures are able to grow larger than land animals with exoskeletons. This is because sea water helps to support the weight of an animal's body.

Scuttling and scooting

Crustaceans move in a number of ways. Crabs scuttle sideways along the shore or seabed. Lobsters can swim only forwards or backwards. They paddle in the water or, for a quicker escape, flick their tail under their body. The action pushes water forwards, and drives the lobster backwards in a flash. Both crabs and lobsters have fearsome claws with serrated pincers. The animals use these to fight their enemies, grab their prey, and crush or tear it apart.

A new suit

Like all animals with exoskeletons, crustaceans have to shed their skin, or moult, in order to grow. When a crab moults, cracks appear in its shell and the soft body underneath starts to push its way out. This is a dangerous time for the crab: its soft body is very easy for enemies to attack. During the moult, the crab has to hide itself away while its new exoskeleton hardens.

Left A spider crab has five pairs of long legs. Each leg is made of tubes of exoskeleton, linked at the joints.

Spiny carapace
Joint

Right A crab's exoskeleton is made mainly of chitin. On top, the animal is covered by a stronger material, which forms a hard shield called the **carapace**.

Back legs for walking
Claws for fighting and feeding
Eye
Carapace

THE BIG BOOK OF BONES 13

Left A tiny shrimp scoots backwards with a flick of the tail. It can also use its legs as paddles.

Below Lobsters and crabs are delicious to eat when cooked. But before you can eat the soft, tasty meat, you have to crack open the hard casing with special tools.

Below A lobster is like a very large shrimp. It can grow up to 75 cm.

Strong armourplating

Five pairs of jointed legs

Pincers have one knobbly, crushing claw and one sharp, cutting claw

BONE UP!

- There are 38,000 different crustaceans. Some are microscopic.
- A lobster's claws are strong enough to snap off a human finger or toe.
- Lobsters are dark blue when they are alive, but turn red when they are cooked.
- After moulting, many crabs eat their nutritious old skin.
- Many crustaceans are small. The pea crab is tiny – just the size of a pea.
- A crab's hard shell doesn't always save it from enemies. Octopuses, birds, seals and some fish all eat crabs.
- If a crab loses a claw in a fight, it will grow a new one.
- The woodlouse is the only crustacean that lives on dry land.

INSIDE A SHELL

Many sea creatures live inside a shell: this is another kind of skeleton. Most shelled animals, such as mussels, oysters, clams and whelks, belong to a group called **molluscs**. Their shells come in many shapes and sizes. Some are extremely graceful, with a glossy shine, fine markings and a pearly inner lining. But even the plainest shell is a life-saver, protecting its owner from being eaten by enemies, pounded by waves, or crushed on the rocks.

Building a home

Each seashell is made by the creature inside it. The animal produces a chalky material called calcium carbonate, which slowly builds into layers of shell. Its shape depends on how much calcium carbonate is released from each side of the animal's body. Week by week, the shell grows larger, providing extra space for the growing animal. The expanding shell is safer for its owner than an exoskeleton, because it doesn't need to be shed as the creature grows.

Inside a pearly nautilus shell. The curving compartments work like buoyancy tanks. By filling them with either air or water, the nautilus is able to float upwards or downwards in the sea

An Indian volute. This whorl-shaped shell gets bigger as the animal grows

Conch

Abalone shell lined with mother-of-pearl

Marble cone

Harp shell

Cowries

Right These shells were once homes to soft-bodied sea creatures. Shells come in a wonderful variety of shapes and markings: some are small and delicate; others large and heavy.

Skeleton cliffs

Did you know that some cliffs are made of skeletons?

Over millions of years, the shells of microscopic animals built up on the seabed, forming a chalky rock. Movements inside the Earth pushed the rock upwards to form chalk cliffs, such as the famous white cliffs at Dover.

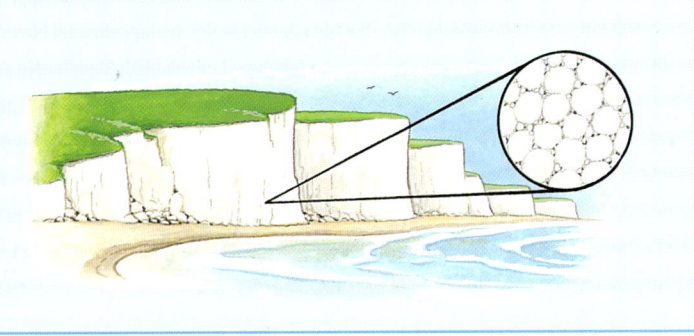

Moving about

Some molluscs, such as razorshells, oysters and mussels, have two matching shells, and are called **bivalves**. Because they cannot move around easily, many bivalves cling to rocks or burrow deep down in the sand. Scallops, however, shoot through the water by opening and closing their shells. Other molluscs, such as sea snails, have only one shell, which usually grows in a spiral shape made up of **whorls**. These animals move more easily than bivalves, crawling over seaweed, sand or rock. Limpets have a simple, cap-shaped shell and fix themselves to rocks when the tide is out. As soon as the tide comes in, they release their grip and move slowly over the rock.

One kind of nautilus makes a thin, papery shell for its eggs

A cockle's thick, ribbed shells are extra strong

The bramble murex has a ridge of spines

Limpets have a single shell

Above Bivalves have two matching shells. The animals' strong muscles can close the shells so tightly that they're almost impossible for a predator to open. These queen scallops open their shells to breathe and feed. As water filters in, the scallops take in oxygen and feed on microscopic creatures. (Notice the barnacles that have attached themselves to the upper shells. Barnacles are crustaceans.)

BONE UP!

- Hundreds of years ago, people in the Pacific Islands and parts of Africa used shells as money.
- Some molluscs, such as slugs and snails, live on land.
- Some shells have a pearly coating inside them called nacre. Most people know it as mother-of-pearl.
- The deep-sea clam is the slowest growing animal in the world. It takes a hundred years to grow just 8 mm – about the size of a human toenail.

SKELETONS IN THE SEA

In the warm, shallow waters of tropical oceans live small sea creatures called corals. They live in huge colonies, containing millions of tiny animals. Each animal is called a polyp. It has a soft body which produces a chalky substance that hardens into a cup shape, in which the polyp is fixed. The cup does the job of a skeleton, protecting the animal from damaging sea currents and hungry fish. To feed, the polyp stretches out its tentacles to trap small animals and plants.

Below A coral reef is like a sheltered, underwater village inhabited by fish, starfish, octopuses, sponges, and many other creatures. This coral reef in Malaysia is a safe nursery for young fish.

Above Coral reefs are made of the hard skeletons of tiny polyps. This is a branch coral.

THE BIG BOOK OF BONES   17

An octopus's garden

When polyps die, their tiny skeletons remain. Millions of them gradually build up to form huge structures which are as hard as stone. These are called coral reefs.

Coral reefs look like underwater gardens, full of colour, shape and variety. Corals grow in hundreds of different ways. Some form round pads like cushions. Others look like plants, with waving branches and fan-like twigs. They form a unique habitat for many different forms of life.

The world's largest coral reef is the Great Barrier Reef, off Australia. It forms a line of underwater hills over 2000 km long.

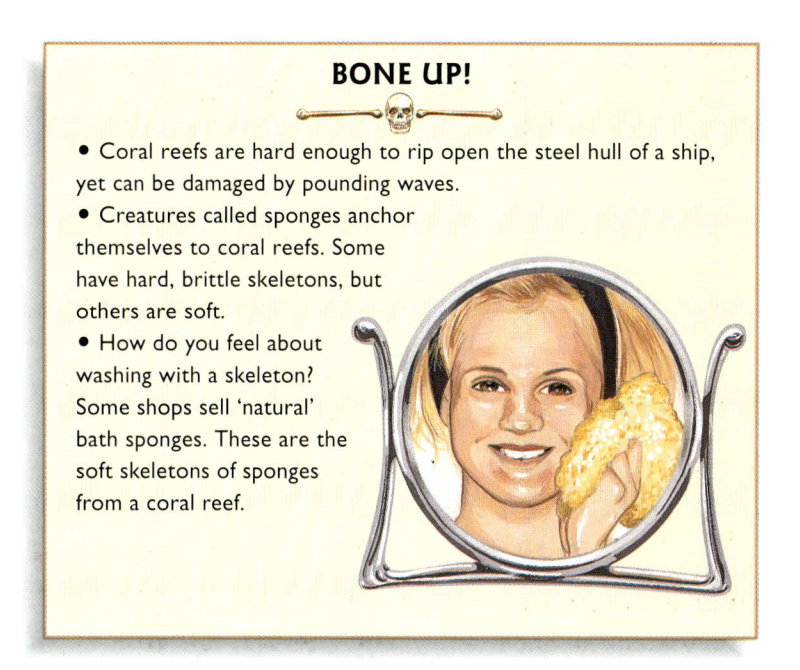

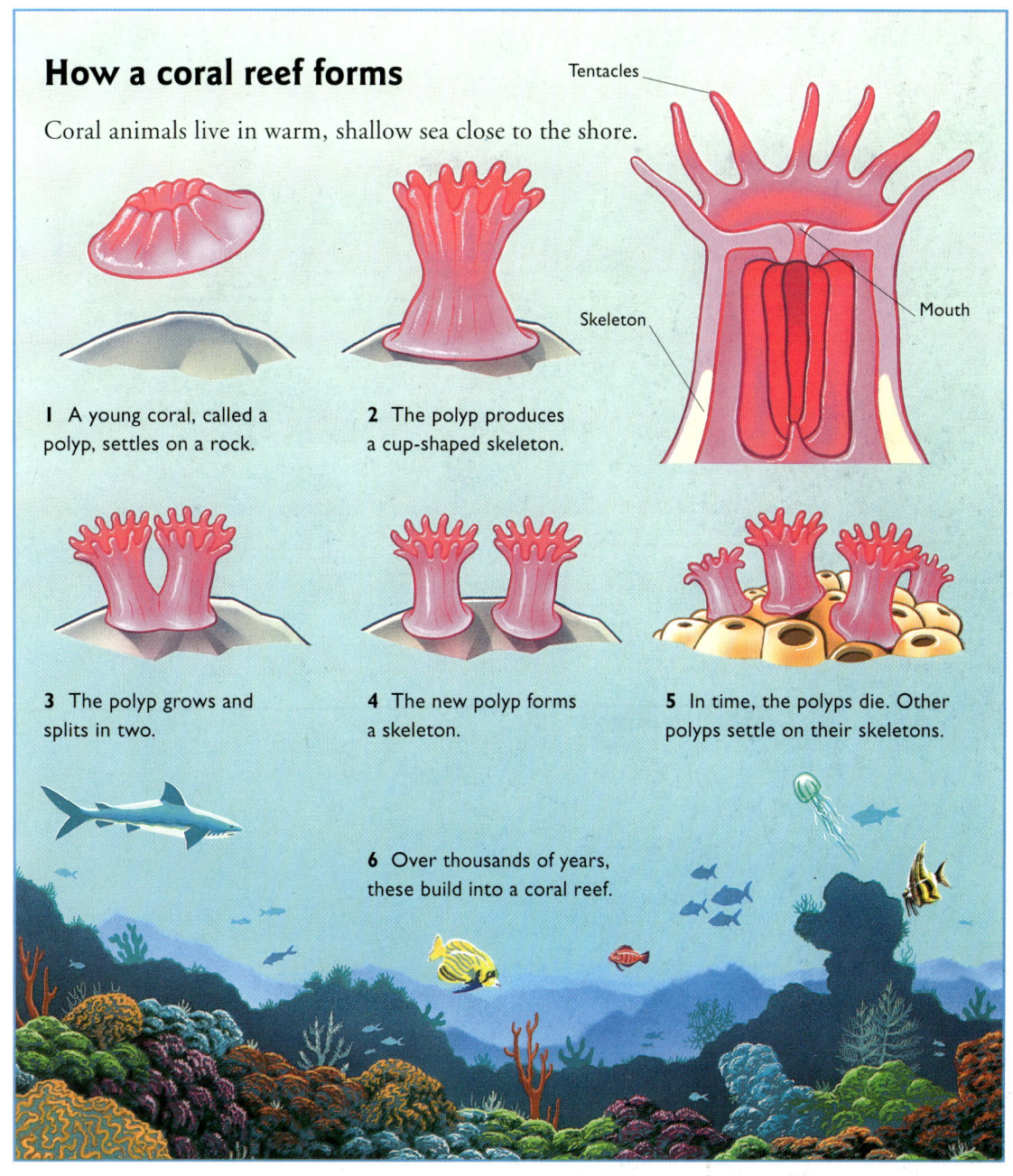

BONE UP!

- Coral reefs are hard enough to rip open the steel hull of a ship, yet can be damaged by pounding waves.
- Creatures called sponges anchor themselves to coral reefs. Some have hard, brittle skeletons, but others are soft.
- How do you feel about washing with a skeleton? Some shops sell 'natural' bath sponges. These are the soft skeletons of sponges from a coral reef.

How a coral reef forms

Coral animals live in warm, shallow sea close to the shore.

1 A young coral, called a polyp, settles on a rock.

2 The polyp produces a cup-shaped skeleton.

3 The polyp grows and splits in two.

4 The new polyp forms a skeleton.

5 In time, the polyps die. Other polyps settle on their skeletons.

6 Over thousands of years, these build into a coral reef.

FISH BONES

Fish appeared on Earth about 500 million years ago. They were the very first **vertebrates**: the earliest creatures to have a backbone, or spine. Up until then, all animals had been invertebrates. The backbone was an important development in the animal kingdom. This long line of bones ran the whole length of the body, and was tough but flexible. It provided a strong structure for the body, and gave the muscles something to pull on. It really got animals moving!

Bone and gristle

Most fish have a bony skeleton. A few fish, such as sharks and rays, have a skeleton made of cartilage (the gristly material in your nose and ears). Cartilage isn't as strong as bone, and couldn't carry the weight of a land animal. But weight is less of a problem in the sea, where the water gives extra support.

A smooth mover

The skeleton of a fish is simple in design, with a skull, backbone and tail. There are no hips, shoulders or limbs to break up its smooth profile. This sleek streamlining helps fish to move swiftly and easily. Muscles along each side of the body pull on the spine, bending it from side to side. This waving movement pushes the fish through the water. Meanwhile, the fan-shaped fins keep the fish upright and allow it to change direction.

Fins control rolling when swimming

Bony plates protect head

Eye socket

Tail fin powers fish along

Spine/backbone

Jaws

Skull bones

Above The perch is a typical bony fish. Its skeleton is made up of three parts: the skull, the long backbone and ribs, and the bony spikes that support the fins.

Tail fin

Spine/backbone

Right The flounder's wider skeleton shows that it is not a fast swimmer. Flounders are flatfish that lie on the seabed. As the young develop, their skull and jaw twist round, and the left eye joins the right on one side.

Ribs

Space for internal organs

Eyes face upwards, looking for enemies

THE BIG BOOK OF BONES 19

Above A sand tiger shark. Most sharks are built for speed. Their bodies are supported by cartilage, which is lighter and more flexible than bone.

Jaws and teeth

Jaws give important clues to diet. Barracudas, sharks and piranhas are hunters, and have a mouthful of razor-sharp teeth. The porcupine fish has large, flattened teeth which are perfect for crushing shellfish. The whale shark gulps in water through its wide mouth, and traps microscopic plants and animals in packed rows of tiny teeth.

BONE UP!

- Fish were the first animals to have jaws. Before then, animals could only suck food. They couldn't bite or chew.
- Sharks never stop growing new teeth. The teeth are stacked up in rows, and move forward as old ones wear out. Each tooth lasts just eight to ten days.

How do fish swim?

1 A dogfish swims by squeezing, or contracting, the muscles on each side of its body, starting at the head.

2 As the muscles contract, they pull on the backbone to create a curve, first on one side of the body, and then on the other.

3 The waving movement drives the fish forwards. It achieves an extra push by beating its tail from side to side.

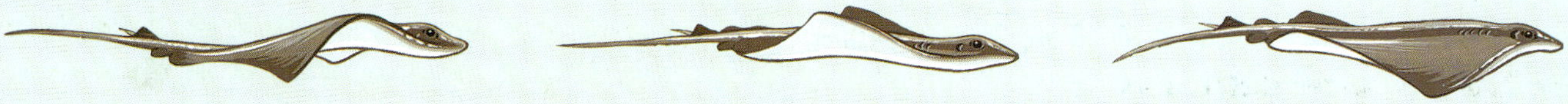

1 A ray has a flattened body, with huge fins on the side.

2 To swim, it flaps its fins just like a bird flaps its wings.

3 This creates a waving, up-and-down movement that forces the fish forwards.

Rugged Reptiles

Reptiles are mainly land animals. They have a bony skeleton, often with a small skull, a long, flexible backbone and tail, and most of them have four legs that stick out from the sides. But reptile skeletons are not all the same.

Lizards
Lizards make up the largest group of reptiles, and come in many different sizes. Lizards' short legs make them look like they are doing press-ups! Lizards tend to run and stop, run and stop – they're taking a moment to rest.

Crocodiles and alligators
Crocodiles and alligators spend much of their time in water. Their long tail makes a powerful paddle that drives them along very quickly. They have a large, strong skull, and their nostrils and eyes sit high on the head. This means that they can breathe easily and keep a lookout for prey while lying half-hidden in the water.

Tortoises and turtles
Tortoises and turtles are unique in the animal kingdom because they have both an exoskeleton (in most cases, a horny shell), and an endoskeleton made of bone. The two skeletons are joined together under the shell, and cannot be separated. They make an impenetrable fortress which provides great protection, but the shell is so heavy that tortoises are some of the slowest-moving animals on Earth.

Above and below Like many lizards, chameleons are at home in bushes and trees. They move very slowly, gripping on tightly with their long, curving toes.

Above Terrapins have flippers to swim with, instead of feet. Their hard shell covers the whole body except for their head, flippers and tail.

THE BIG BOOK OF BONES 21

Snakes

Snakes have no legs at all. Their skeletons are little more than a skull, a long, curving backbone and a body-length tunnel of ribs. Like all vertebrates, a snake's backbone is made up of small bones called **vertebrae** (up to 400 of them), which work like the links in a chain. Each vertebra can only move a little, but a line of them can bend into loops and coils.

Snakes move by using their strong muscles to pull on their backbone, which throws the body into S-shaped curves. Many snakes also swim, climb trees and burrow under the ground.

Right This X-ray of a snake shows its long, sinuous backbone. The bulge in the snake's middle is a frog it has recently caught and eaten.

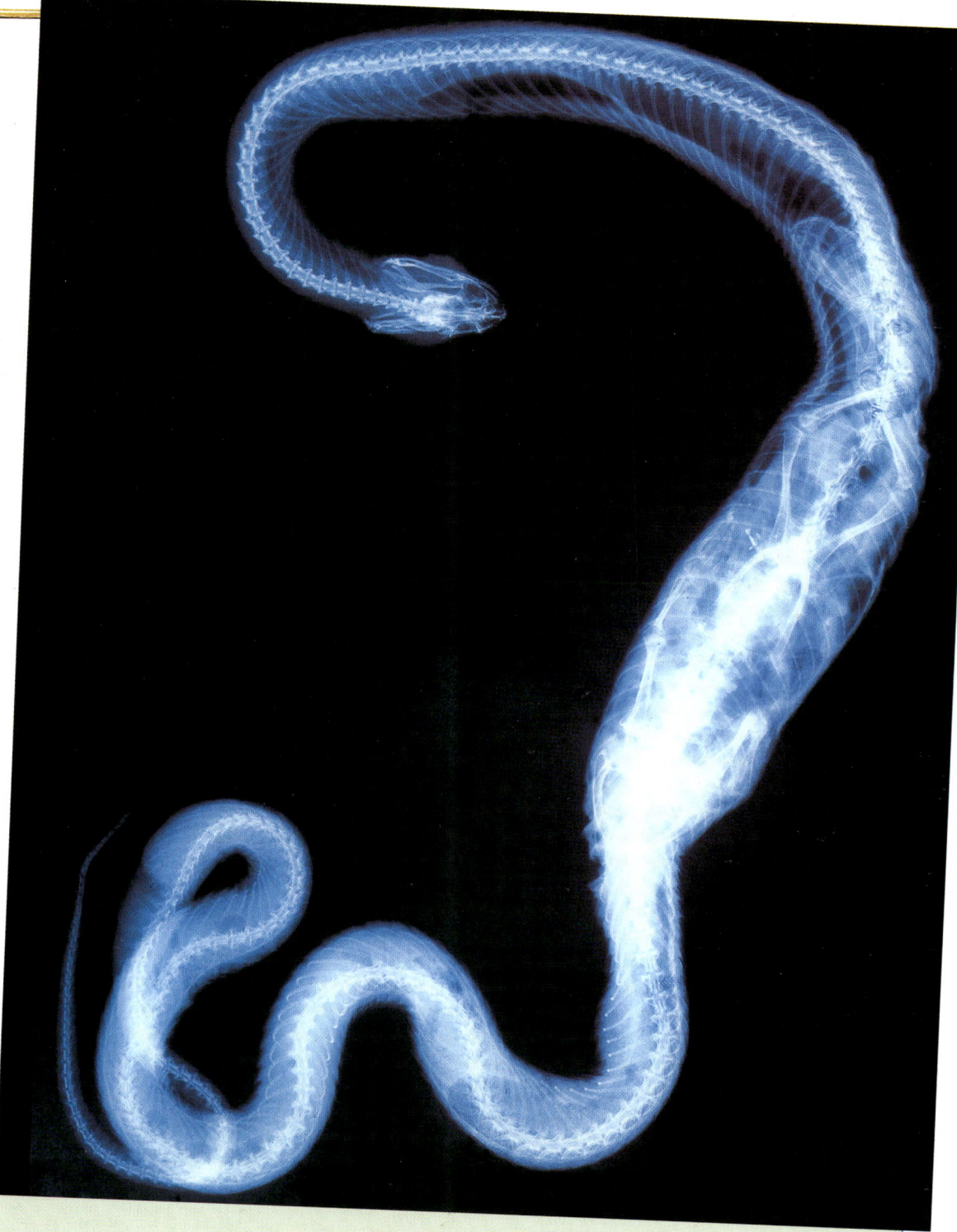

A monster meal

A snake can eat a meal as large as a deer, which it swallows in a single mouthful. How does it manage to do it?

A snake's jaws are joined at the sides of its head by a bony hinge. The hinge 'unhooks', allowing the mouth to open much wider. The bottom jaw is made in two parts, which are joined at the chin by a stretchy ligament. This helps the jaw to e-x-p-a-n-d sideways.

A snake stretches its mouth over its food and swallows it headfirst. Once the meal is inside the snake's mouth, its teeth grip hold of the food and move it backwards towards the throat, where it is swallowed.

Flying Skeletons

Birds are expert fliers. Their skeletons have developed in special ways to make them as light as possible, and yet strong enough to fly long distances in all kinds of weather. A bird's bones are hollow, and strengthened inside by struts. And it has a lightweight beak of horn instead of heavy jawbones and teeth.

On the wing

Over millions of years, birds **evolved** from reptiles, and their front legs developed into wings. The framework of bones inside a wing is similar in pattern to a human arm and hand. It is the feathers, attached to the bones by muscles, that create the shape of the wing. A long-distance flier such as the swift has curved, pointed wings for speed and strength; a seabird such as the gull has long, slim wings that glide on the breeze. Every bird's wings are powered by strong flight muscles. These are anchored to a broad slab of bone under the bird's breast.

Above A bird's wing bones are similar to those found in the human arm.

Below The wing movements of a blue tit in flight.

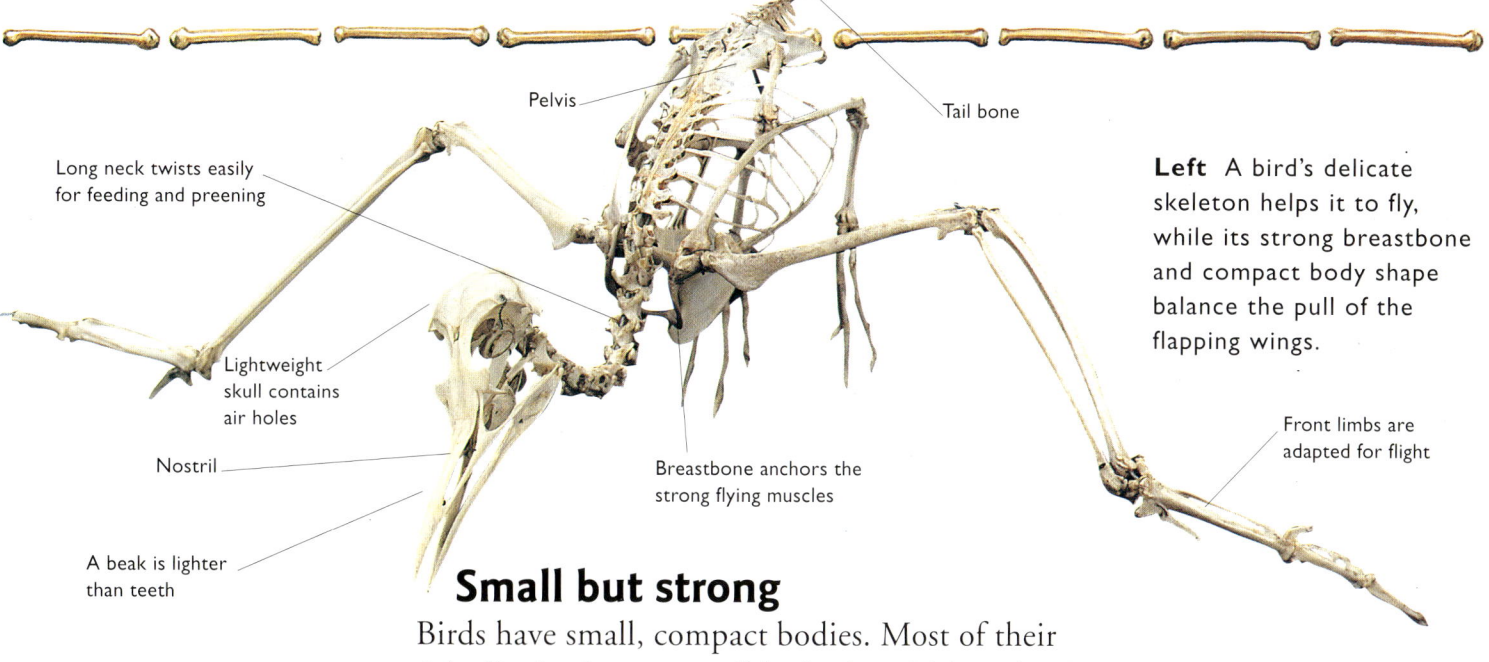

THE BIG BOOK OF BONES 23

Pelvis
Tail bone
Long neck twists easily for feeding and preening
Lightweight skull contains air holes
Nostril
Breastbone anchors the strong flying muscles
A beak is lighter than teeth
Front limbs are adapted for flight

Left A bird's delicate skeleton helps it to fly, while its strong breastbone and compact body shape balance the pull of the flapping wings.

Small but strong

Birds have small, compact bodies. Most of their weight lies in the centre of the body, which makes it easier for them to balance both on land and in the air. Also, unlike most animals, their backbone is short and stiff, which makes them stronger and more stable as they fly. Their neck, however, is long and flexible. It helps them to reach food and to twist as they preen their feathers.

Below Some birds cannot fly, and their skeletons have developed differently. Ostriches have solid bones, and long, strong legs and feet. These huge, heavy birds can run quickly.

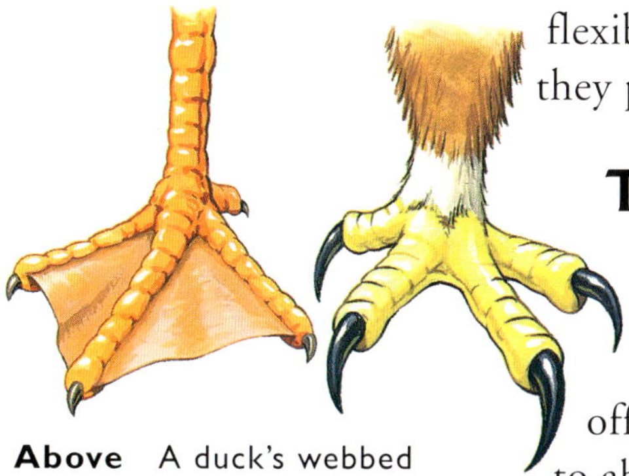

Above A duck's webbed feet (left) make paddles in the water; an eagle's sharp talons (right) catch and kill its prey.

Toes and talons

Birds have sturdy, flexible legs. They use them not only to walk, but to push off the ground at take-off, and to absorb the impact of landing. Birds' feet vary, depending on where and how they live. A sparrow's curling toes cling on to branches. A moorhen's long, splayed toes stop it sinking into soft, gooey mud.

Brilliant beaks

Birds do not have teeth, and use their beaks as tools to catch and grasp their food. The length and shape of a bird's beak are designed for the food it eats. Seed-eaters, such as finches, have strong, short beaks to crack open hard seedcases. Flamingos wade in lakes to find food. Their beaks contain a kind of sieve, which traps tiny creatures in the water. Owls and other birds of prey have hooked beaks to rip their catch apart. A bird also uses its beak to clean its feathers. This is important for keeping it in tip-top flying condition.

Above An oystercatcher's long beak (top) probes for worms in the mud; a finch's beak (bottom) cracks open seeds easily.

BONE UP!

• The smallest living bird is the bee hummingbird. It weighs less than a sugar cube. The African ostrich is the largest and heaviest living bird, and weighs as much as 125 bags of sugar.
• Birds have powerful muscles. Some ducks can fly 1,600 km in a single day.
• Ostriches can run about 65 km/h – that's faster than a racehorse.
• A blackbird weighs only 100 g – about the same as a small apple.

Monster and Mini Mammals

There are over 4,000 different kinds of mammal, ranging in size from a tiny shrew to a mighty whale. And yet their skeletons are remarkably similar. Usually, they have a skull, a single jawbone, a strong, flexible backbone and four limbs. Most mammals have exactly the same bones throughout their body, but some (such as the limb bones) have developed in different ways. These changes took place over millions of years, depending on where and how an animal lived.

Walkers

Most mammals live on land. Unlike mammals living in the sea (which are supported by the water) their long backbone carries the entire weight of the body, like a strong steel girder in a building. The body is raised off the ground by four sturdy legs. The size, shape and arrangement of the foot and leg bones,

Below A monkey's long arms and legs show that it spends a lot of time up in the trees.

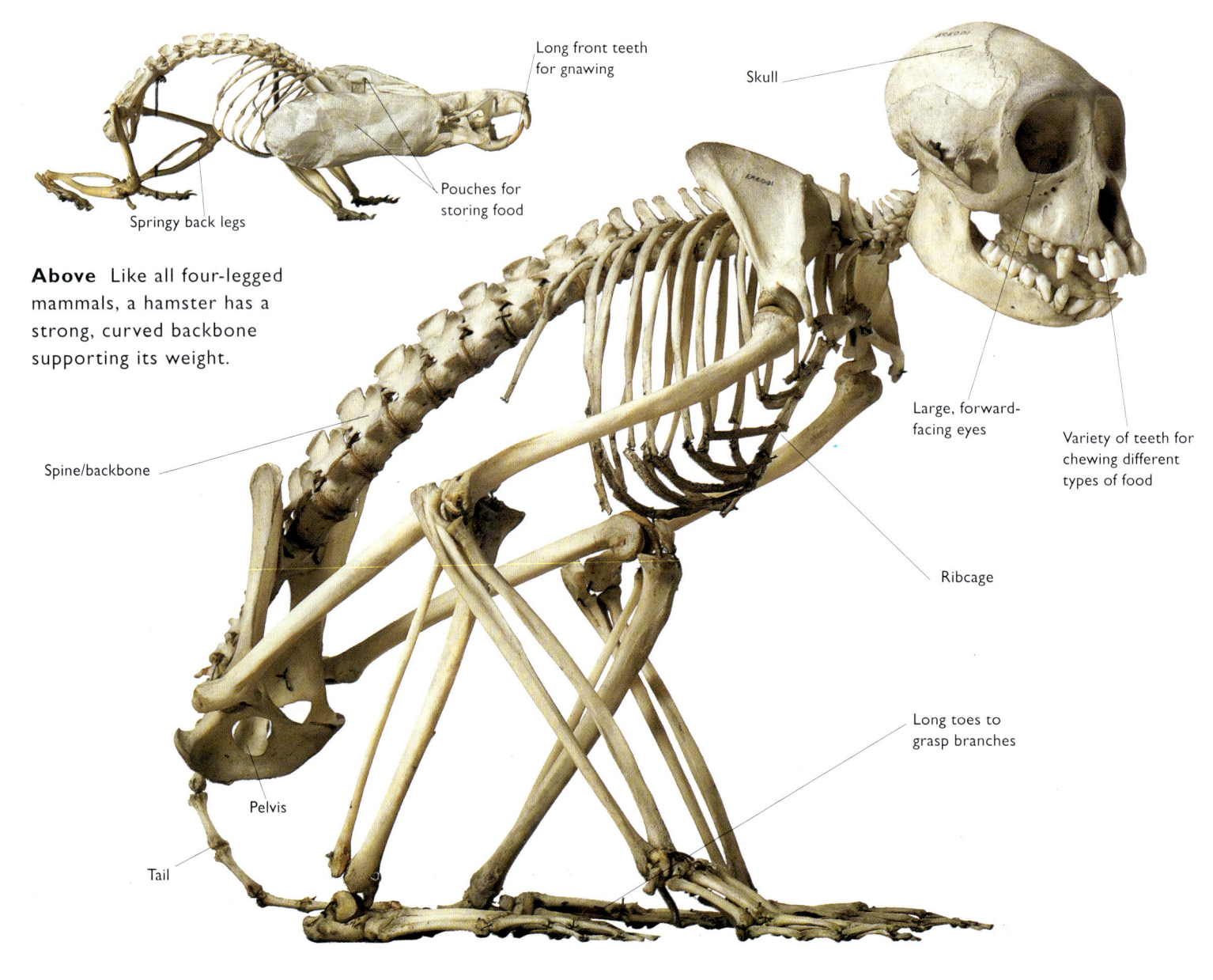

Above Like all four-legged mammals, a hamster has a strong, curved backbone supporting its weight.

- Long front teeth for gnawing
- Pouches for storing food
- Springy back legs
- Spine/backbone
- Pelvis
- Tail
- Skull
- Large, forward-facing eyes
- Variety of teeth for chewing different types of food
- Ribcage
- Long toes to grasp branches

THE BIG BOOK OF BONES 25

Left The skeleton of a mammoth, an elephant-like mammal which lived in North America over 10,000 years ago. It was built like a bridge, with an arched backbone supported by two pairs of legs. This robust framework held up the animal's heavy body, and the massive skull supported its long, curved tusks.

and the way these connect at the ankles and hips, determine the way that a mammal walks: on its toes or its heels, on four legs or two.

Swimmers and fliers

The first mammals were land animals but, in time, some took to the air or moved to the sea. Their skeletons, particularly the limbs, adapted in very different ways. Bats developed thin arms and long fingers, which when covered by skin, formed wings. Seals and sea lions developed extra-long toes and fingers, which formed flippers to swim with.

BONE UP!

- The first whales had tiny back legs, but these have now disappeared.
- Like most mammals, you too have a tail. It's a tiny knob of bone called the coccyx, which lies at the base of your spine.
- Some mammal skeletons come with ready-made weapons, such as pointed antlers, curving horns, or long, ivory tusks.
- An elephant's legs are so solid and strong that the animal can sleep standing up, without danger of falling over.

Above A blue whale is twenty times heavier than an elephant, yet has a much lighter skeleton because its body is supported by water.

The Human Skeleton
Skull to Hips

Like fish, birds, reptiles and other mammals, humans have a bony skeleton inside their body. The bottom half of the skeleton – from the hips to the feet – allows us to walk upright. The top half includes the skull, arms and hands: our equipment for seeing, hearing, smelling, touching and tasting.

Walking tall

The two halves of the skeleton are linked together by the backbone, which is also called the spine. Most animals walk on four legs, and so their spine is horizontal. But humans walk on two legs, and so the spine is upright, supporting us as we stand. And yet the spine is not straight like a tentpole. Looked at from the side, it forms a curving S-shape. This shape helps to strengthen the spine, and absorbs jolts when we walk or run. It also helps to balance the top half of the body over the hips and legs.

Nerve tunnel

The human backbone is built of thirty-three pillar-shaped bones called vertebrae, some of which are fused together. Vertebrae are small at the top of the spine, but get larger and heavier towards the base, where they carry more of the body's weight. Inside each vertebra is a hollow arch. The arches of all these vertebrae line up to form a long, bony tunnel called the spinal or vertebral column. The tunnel contains and protects the spinal cord, a vital nerve that runs down the spine, carrying messages from the brain to the body and back again.

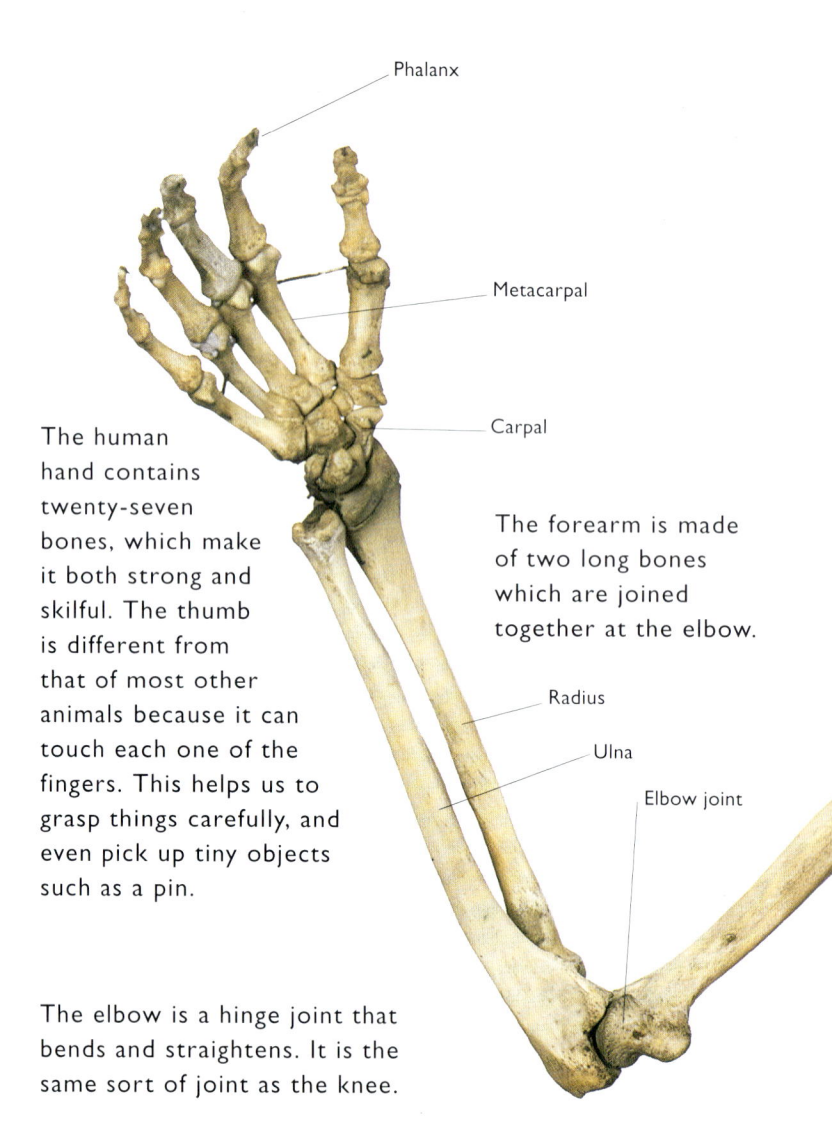

The human hand contains twenty-seven bones, which make it both strong and skilful. The thumb is different from that of most other animals because it can touch each one of the fingers. This helps us to grasp things carefully, and even pick up tiny objects such as a pin.

The forearm is made of two long bones which are joined together at the elbow.

The elbow is a hinge joint that bends and straightens. It is the same sort of joint as the knee.

BONE UP!

- Your 'funny bone' isn't really a bone. It's a sensitive spot on your elbow, where a nerve runs over the end of a bone and passes uncomfortably close to the skin.
- The first seven pairs of ribs are joined at the front to the breastbone (sternum).
- The eighth, ninth and tenth pairs of ribs are joined at the front to the ribs above. They are called false ribs.
- The bottom two pairs of ribs are not joined to anything at the front and are called 'floating ribs'.

THE BIG BOOK OF BONES 27

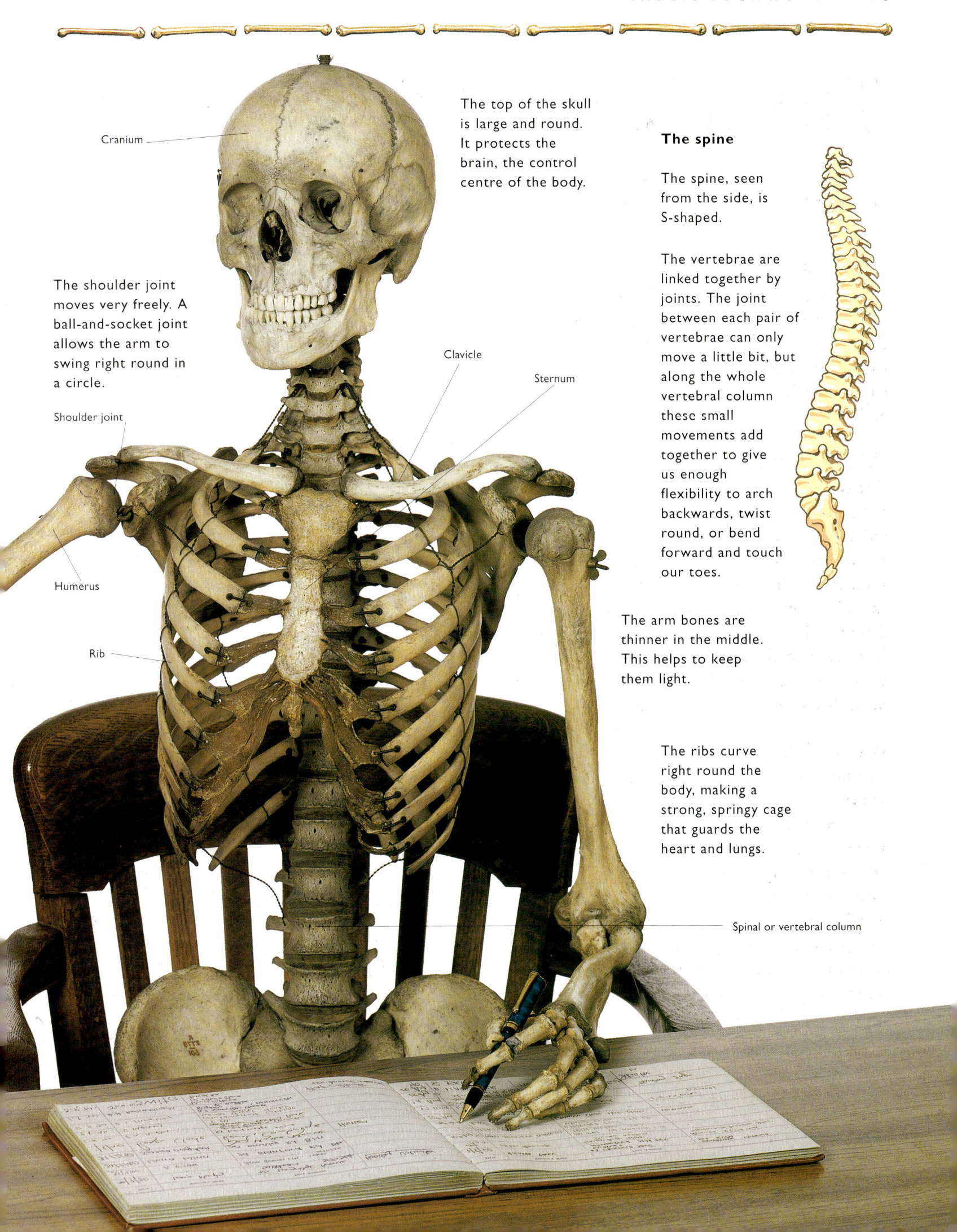

Cranium

The top of the skull is large and round. It protects the brain, the control centre of the body.

The spine

The spine, seen from the side, is S-shaped.

The vertebrae are linked together by joints. The joint between each pair of vertebrae can only move a little bit, but along the whole vertebral column these small movements add together to give us enough flexibility to arch backwards, twist round, or bend forward and touch our toes.

The shoulder joint moves very freely. A ball-and-socket joint allows the arm to swing right round in a circle.

Shoulder joint

Clavicle

Sternum

Humerus

Rib

The arm bones are thinner in the middle. This helps to keep them light.

The ribs curve right round the body, making a strong, springy cage that guards the heart and lungs.

Spinal or vertebral column

THE HUMAN SKELETON
HIPS TO FEET

The bottom half of the skeleton supports us and gets us moving. The legs, our driving force, are connected to the backbone by the pelvis, a bony, bowl-shaped structure.

Baby's cradle

The pelvis is made up of several bones, which join together during early childhood to make a rounded, bony cradle. This protects the soft **intestines** inside the body, and the bladder, where **urine** is stored. In women, the pelvis also protects the **uterus**, where a baby grows. A woman's pelvis is broader and shallower than a man's, and has a wider hole in the middle. This helps when a baby is born, giving it more room to squeeze through.

Weightlifters

Our legs are built from the same basic bones as our arms, but are designed for a very different purpose. While we use our arms to reach out, gather and hold things, we use our legs to carry the body's weight as we stand, walk or run. Because of this, leg bones are longer and thicker than arm bones, and the joints at the hip, knee and ankle are stronger than those at the shoulder, elbow and wrist. This makes our legs stronger but less flexible than our arms.

The human pelvis (this is a man's) is a curved cradle of bone. Its shape helps to keep our legs in line with the top half of our body, improving our overall balance.

Ilium
Ischium
Pubis

The knee joint is the largest joint in the body. Our knees 'lock' firmly when we stand up straight, so our leg muscles don't have to work quite so hard. This makes standing less tiring.

Patella
Tibia
Fibula

BONE UP!

• You can estimate how tall a baby girl will grow by measuring her height at the age of eighteen months, and then doubling it. For a boy, measure his height at the age of two.
• Our distant ancestors had long, flexible toes that they used for gripping – just as apes do today.

THE BIG BOOK OF BONES 29

Pelvis

Sacrum

Coccyx

Hip joint

The hip joint is the strongest joint in the body. The round ball at the top of the thighbone fits snugly inside a deep, cup-shaped socket in the pelvis. It is the same kind of joint as the shoulder, but moves a little less freely.

The coccyx or tailbone is the name given to the three or four vertebrae at the end of the spine. They are a reminder of our far-distant past, when our ancestors probably had tails.

Femur

The thighbone, or femur, is the longest bone in the body. It is roughly as long as the spine, and a quarter of our total height.

Knee joint

Each foot contains twenty-six small bones. They are flatter and longer than the bones in the hands, making it easier for us to balance.

Tarsal

Metatarsal

Phalanx

The Human Skull

When you tap on your head with your knuckles, it makes a hollow sound, like wood. That's because your skull is a bony box. Its hard walls protect the brain inside from damaging knocks and blows.

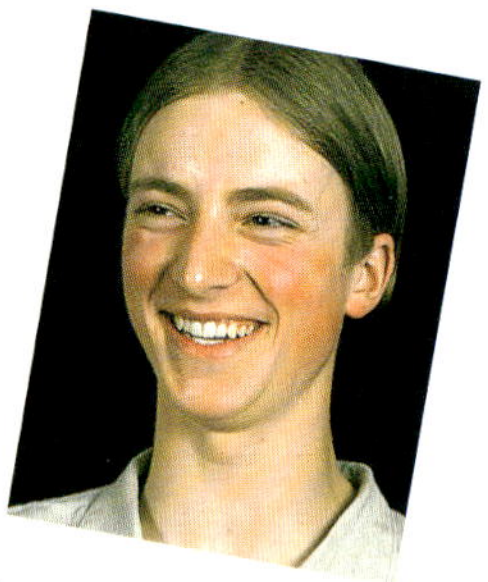

The skull houses four of our five senses: sight, hearing, smell and taste. The eyes are well protected in two bony sockets. The delicate inner ear lies deep inside the skull. Our fleshy nose covers an opening in the skull, where we breathe in air and pick up smells. Our mouth opens and closes on a hinge. The moving jawbone makes an opening where we taste and chew our food before we swallow it.

Skull bones

The skull is a complicated structure, made from twenty-two different bones. Eight curving bones make up the forehead and the big, round dome at the back. This part of the skull is called the **cranium**, and houses the brain. The remaining fourteen bones make up the face. During a child's early years, many of these bones knit together, forming wiggly lines that look like rivers across the skull. They are called sutures. They cannot move, and fade as a person gets older.

Pulling faces

Your face is incredibly mobile. That's because more than thirty muscles lie under the skin, pulling it this way and that. These tiny movements change our expression, and help us to communicate by smiling, looking doubtful, or scowling. The muscles around the mouth are especially important for speech. They pull the lips into various shapes, helping us to make different sounds. The mouth is elastic and never stops moving – just watch someone talking and see.

Orbit (eye socket) Frontal bone Our nose is made of rubbery cartilage, not bone. On a skeleton, all you can see is a hole.

Above The first thing you notice in a skull is the large eye sockets. Our eyes are small, round balls, about the size of golfballs. They are well protected by the forehead above and the cheekbones below.

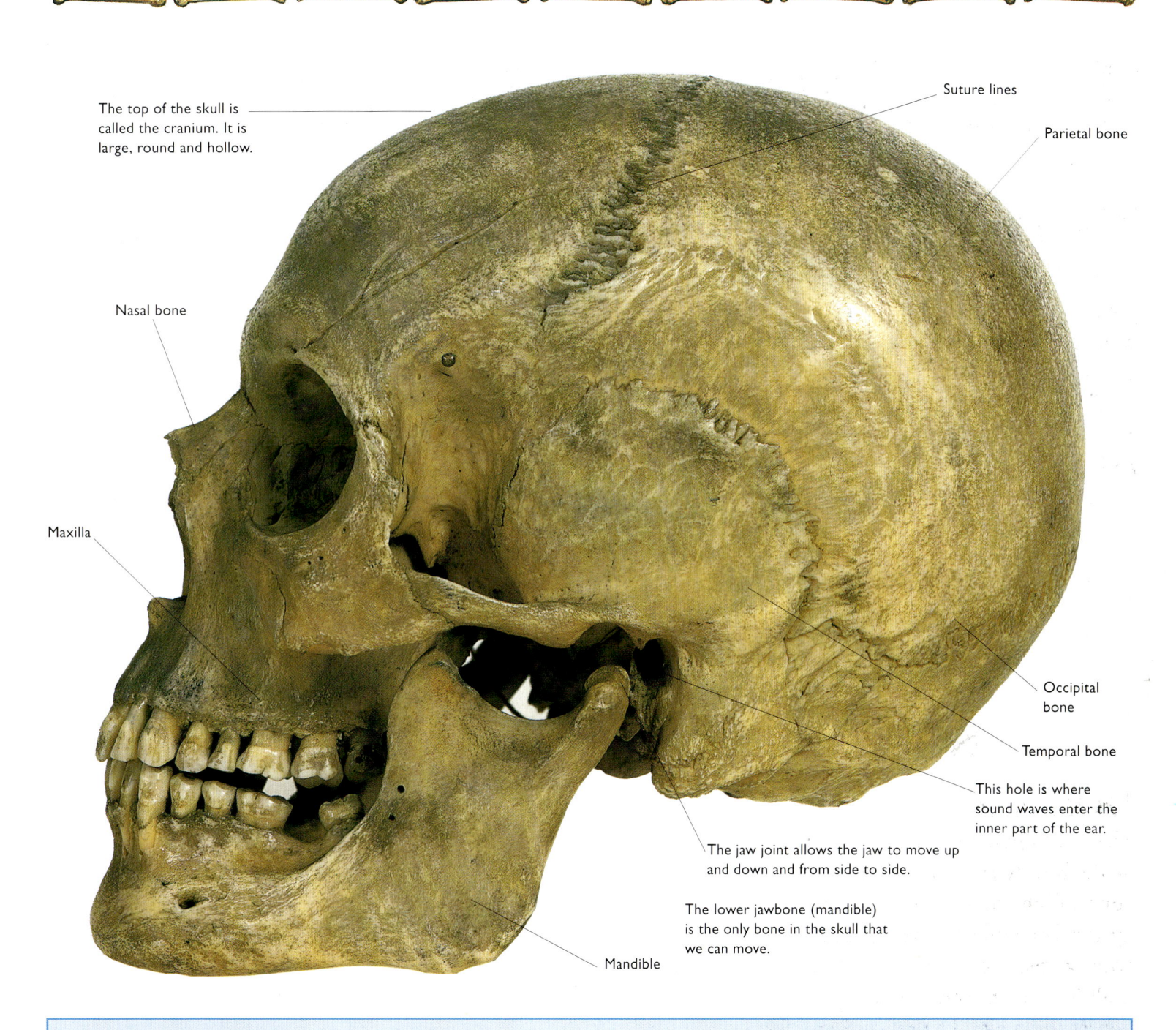

THE BIG BOOK OF BONES 31

The top of the skull is called the cranium. It is large, round and hollow.

Suture lines

Parietal bone

Nasal bone

Maxilla

Occipital bone

Temporal bone

This hole is where sound waves enter the inner part of the ear.

The jaw joint allows the jaw to move up and down and from side to side.

The lower jawbone (mandible) is the only bone in the skull that we can move.

Mandible

A tool kit of teeth

Most babies are born without teeth, but by their third year twenty small 'milk' teeth have grown out through the gums. At about the age of six, these teeth grow loose and start to fall out. Gradually, during the next ten years, thirty-two larger teeth take their place.

Teeth are covered by a hard material called enamel, and have long roots to anchor them in the jawbone. They are various shapes and sizes because many of them do different jobs.

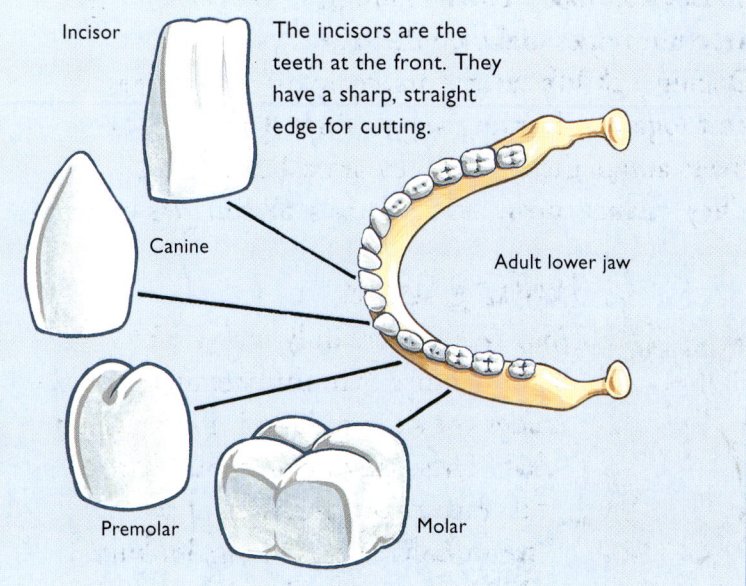

The canine teeth are sharp and pointed to grip and pierce food.

The premolars and molars lie at the back of the mouth. They are broad and flat, and are good at crushing and chewing.

Incisor

The incisors are the teeth at the front. They have a sharp, straight edge for cutting.

Canine

Premolar

Molar

Adult lower jaw

Looking at Bones

To most of us, bones are the dry, white sticks we see in museums. Yet in a living body, bones are nothing of the sort. Bone is moist, living tissue. Just like our skin, it contains blood vessels, nerves, and a mass of busy cells. But bone also contains a substance called calcium, which makes it rigid and hard. This is combined with long, stretchy fibres called collagen. The combination of mainly calcium phosphate and collagen makes bone tough but flexible, like all the best building materials.

Good bone structure

The structure of a bone makes it as strong as steel, but as light as aluminium. On the outside is a hard, dense material known as compact bone. On the inside is a light, honeycomb structure, known as spongy bone, which is strengthened by tiny struts. Spaces in the spongy bone are filled with a soft, jelly-like material called bone marrow, which makes red blood cells. At the centre of long bones, there is a hollow cavity which contains the bone marrow.

Mending a break

Everyone knows someone who has broken a bone. **Fractures** are common injuries caused by awkward movements or accidents. Fortunately, most broken bones knit together easily within six to eight weeks. The bone cells produce extra minerals that bridge the gap between the two broken ends. While this is happening, the bone often needs to be held in place with a splint or plaster cast, so that it grows back straight and strong. But for some serious breaks, the bones have to be fixed together with plates, wires and screws!

On the outside, the materials in the bone are packed together tightly to form dense, compact bone.

Bone marrow cavity

Inside, a criss-cross network of bony struts helps to make bones light but strong.

1 Ouch! Zoe falls awkwardly at football.

2 An ambulance takes her to hospital.

Right
The story of a broken leg! Broken bones are often caused by sports injuries. The broken leg is set in plaster for about six to eight weeks while it mends. Gentle exercise helps it regain its strength, and it's soon as good as new.

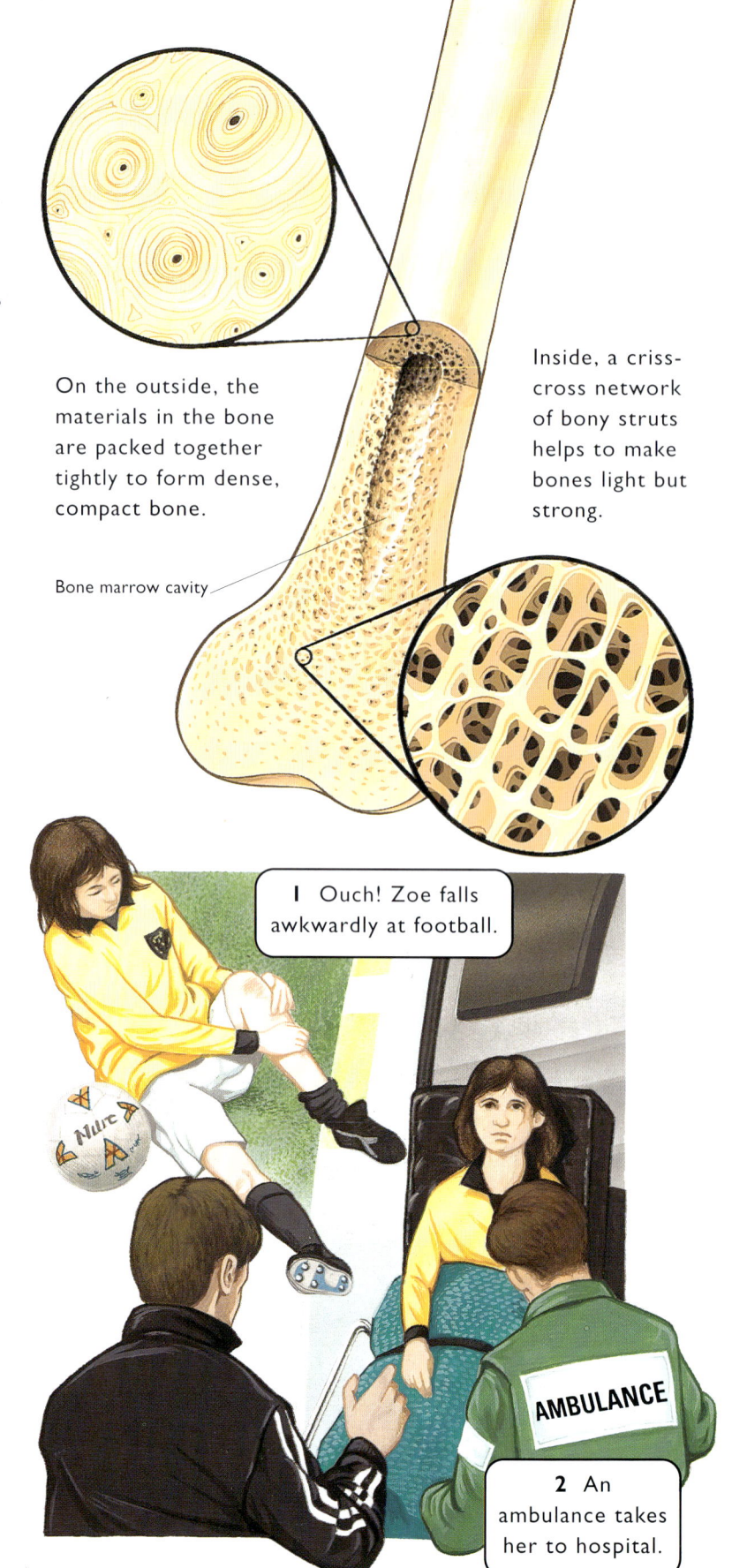

THE BIG BOOK OF BONES **33**

Right X-rays show doctors which bones have been fractured. This X-ray is of a broken arm. Both the forearm bones (the radius and ulna) are fractured, and the sharp broken ends of each bone have separated and are in danger of piercing the skin. This is known as a compound fracture. Bad fractures such as these may need surgery to repair them.

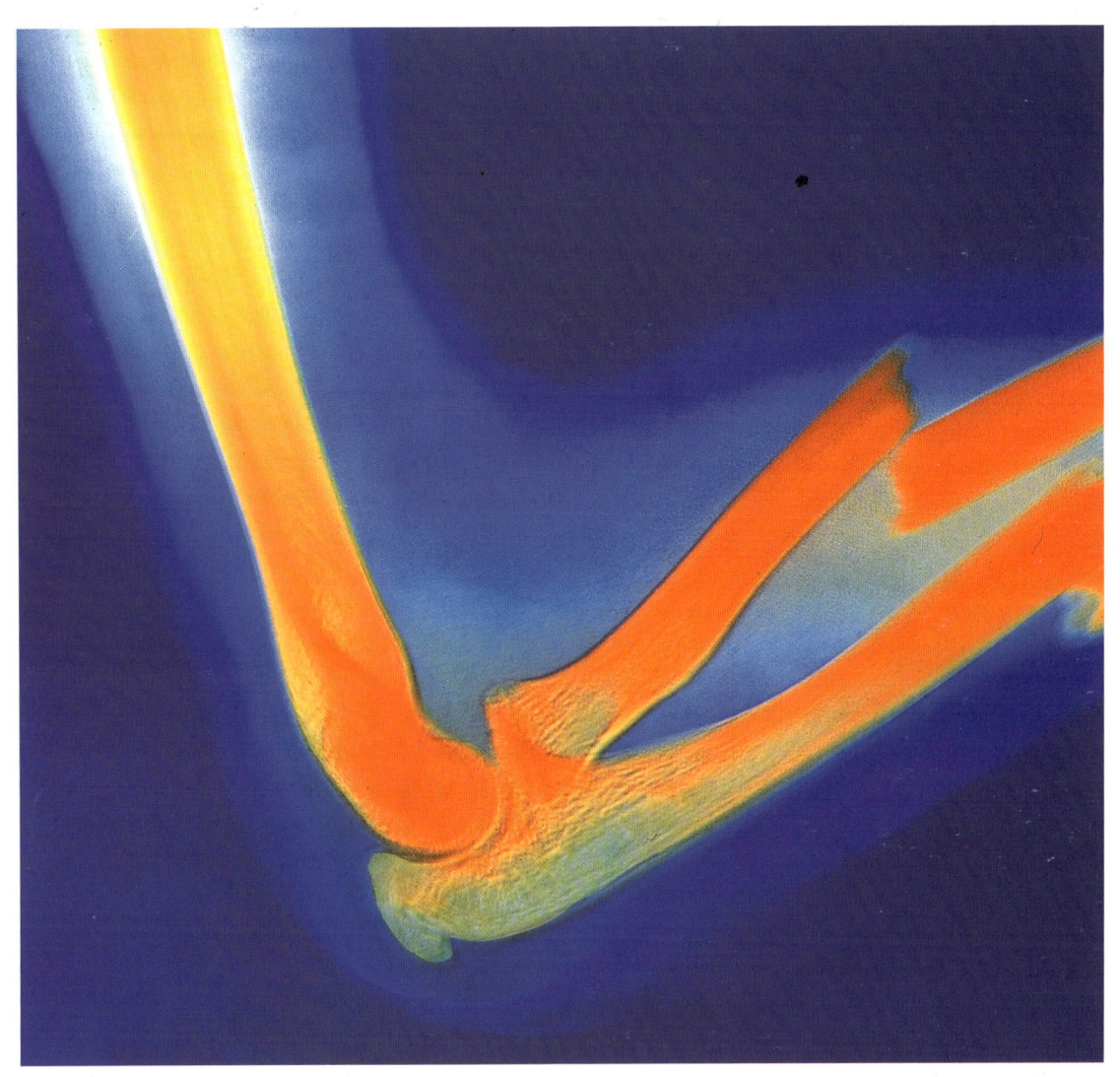

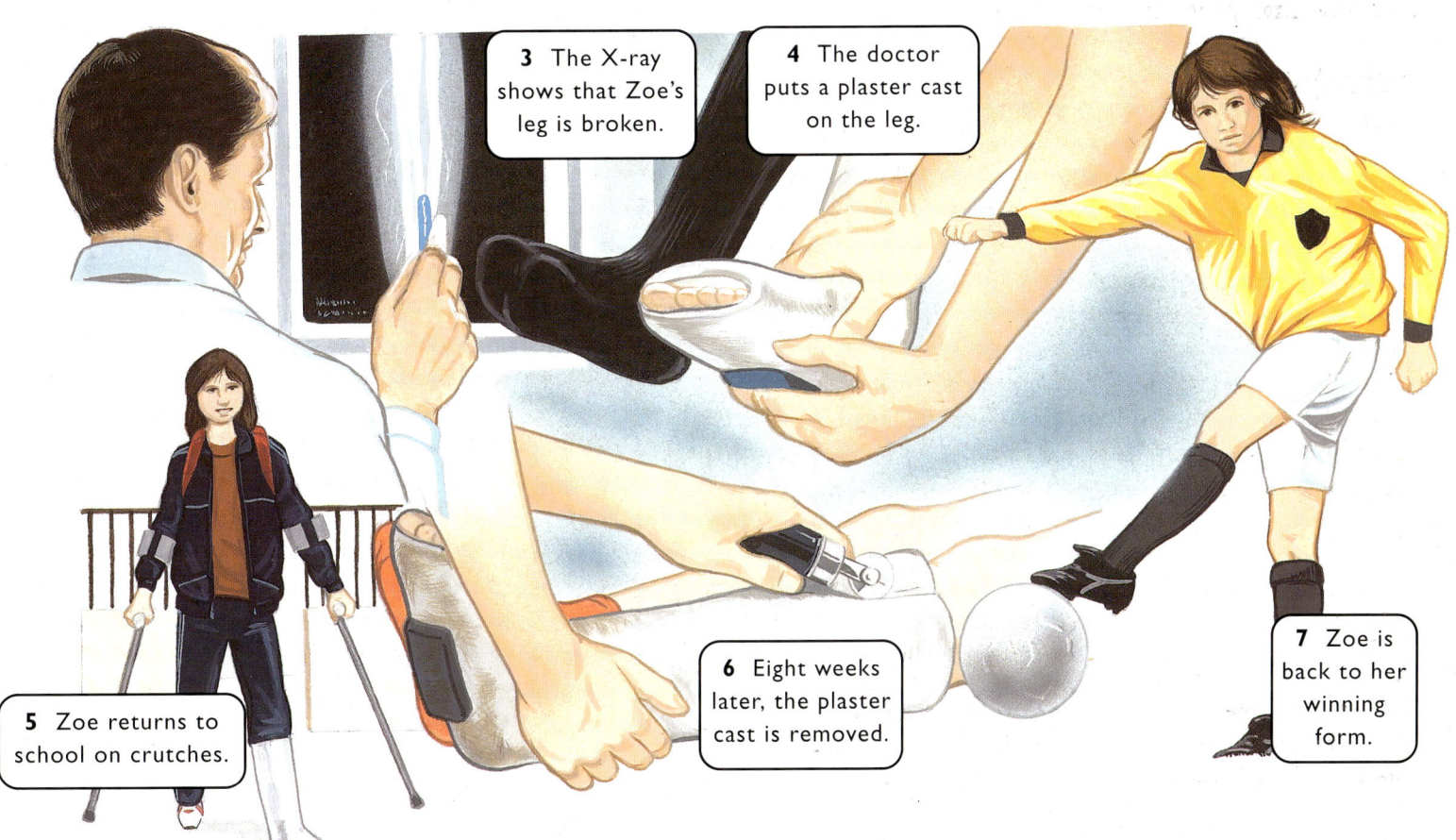

3 The X-ray shows that Zoe's leg is broken.

4 The doctor puts a plaster cast on the leg.

5 Zoe returns to school on crutches.

6 Eight weeks later, the plaster cast is removed.

7 Zoe is back to her winning form.

BONES FOR LIFE

Before birth
For the first nine months of its life, a baby grows inside its mother. It is here that the skeleton starts to form. At first, the skeleton is made of flexible cartilage, but within a few weeks it starts to change. Inside each future bone, cells start to break down the cartilage and replace it with hard calcium phosphate and stretchy collagen, the two main ingredients of bone. This replacement of soft cartilage by hard bone is called **ossification**.

Below A baby can suck its toes because it has a short body and very supple joints.

The growing years
When a baby is born, its skeleton continues to grow, and slowly the rest of the cartilage is replaced by bone. The whole process takes about twenty years. At about the age of six, only the ends of a child's bones still contain cartilage. These parts continue to grow quickly until the child becomes a teenager, and then more slowly, as the teenager becomes an adult.

Bones at work
By about the age of twenty, a person is fully grown and ossification is complete. But even though the body is no longer growing, it is still working hard inside.

Above left This photograph shows an unborn baby, only sixteen weeks old. The lighter areas of the skeleton you can see in the hands, feet and knees, are made of cartilage. The bones in the skull are still separate.

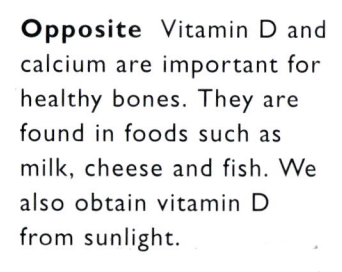

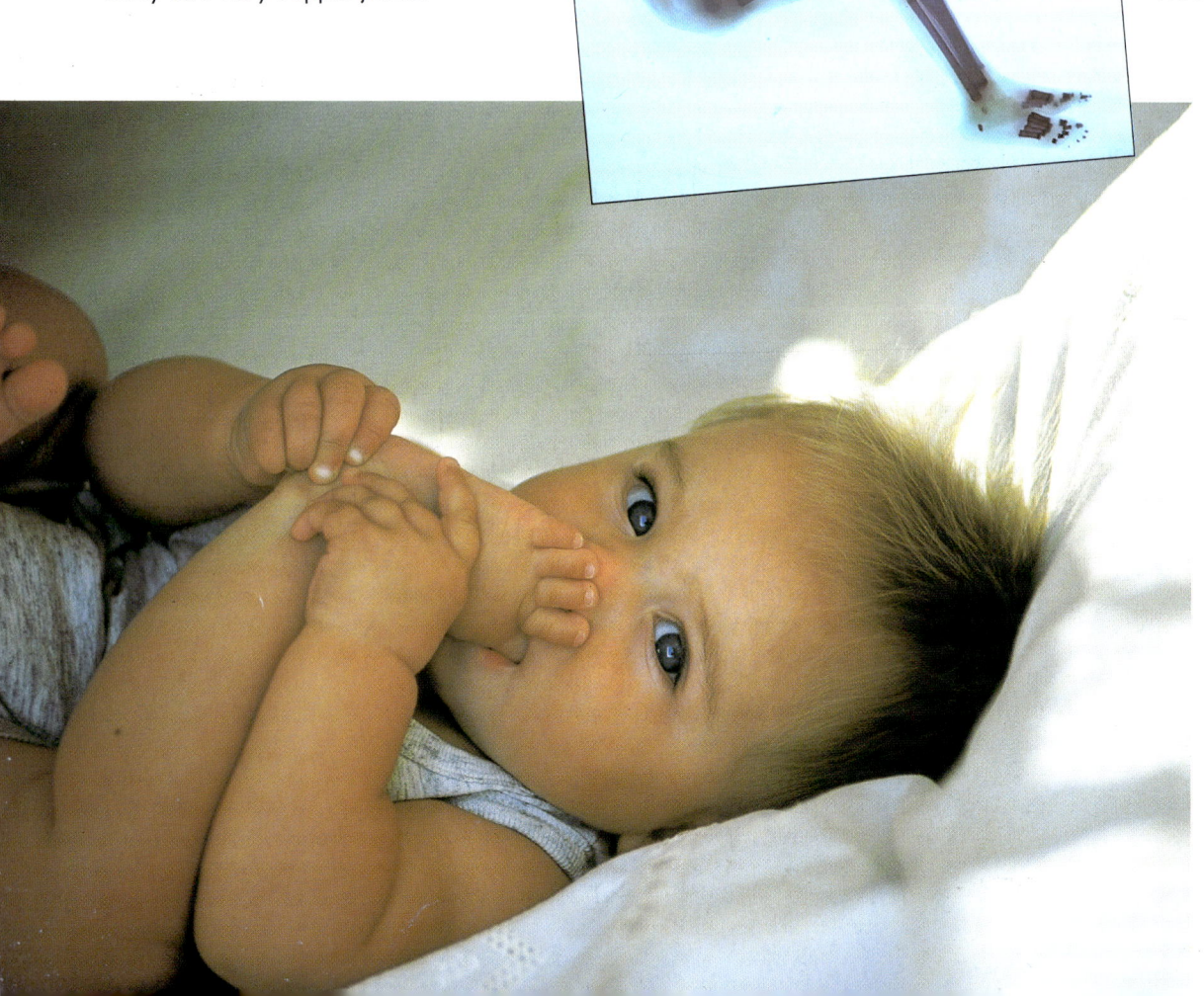

Opposite Vitamin D and calcium are important for healthy bones. They are found in foods such as milk, cheese and fish. We also obtain vitamin D from sunlight.

The bones in the skull

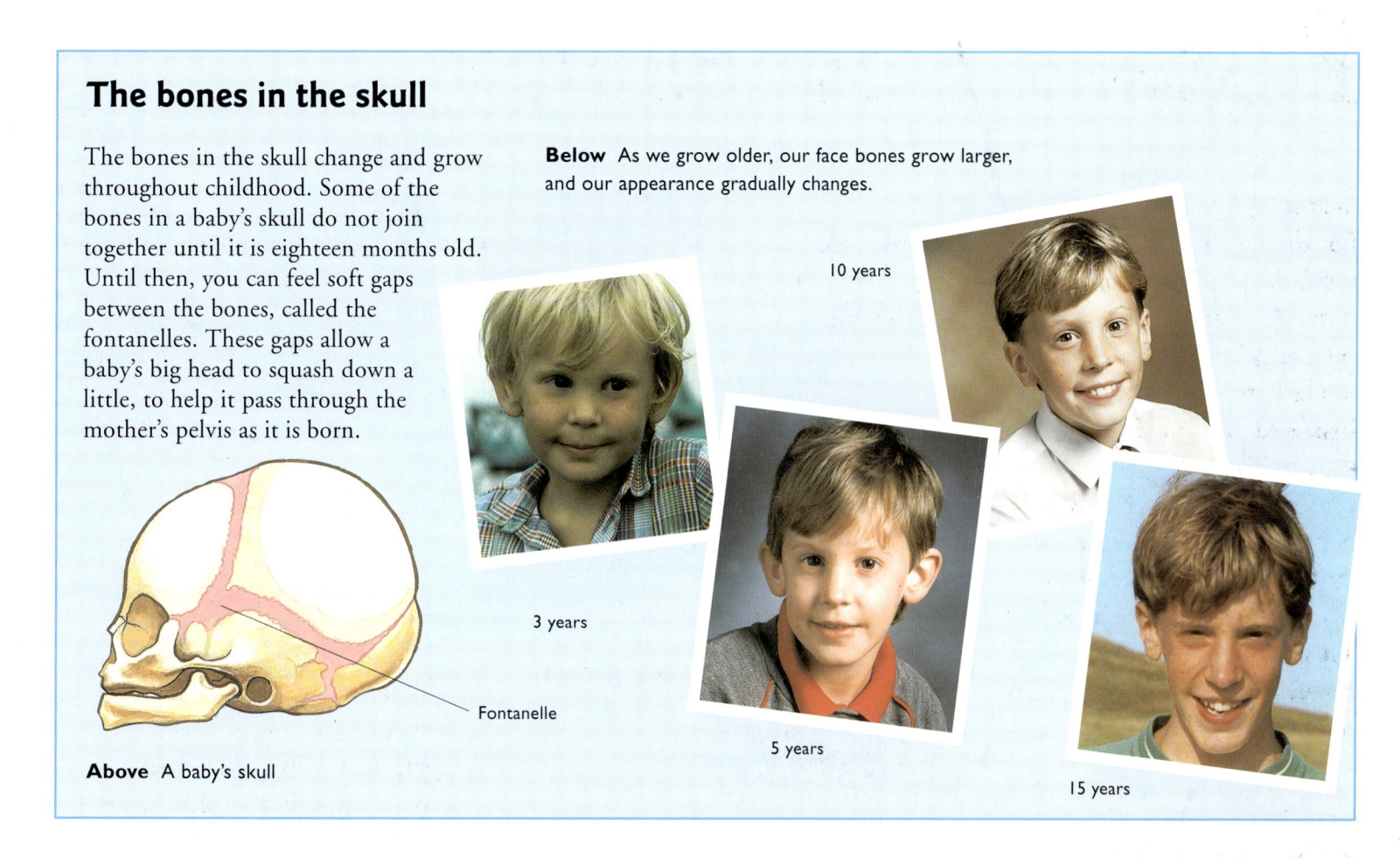

The bones in the skull change and grow throughout childhood. Some of the bones in a baby's skull do not join together until it is eighteen months old. Until then, you can feel soft gaps between the bones, called the fontanelles. These gaps allow a baby's big head to squash down a little, to help it pass through the mother's pelvis as it is born.

Above A baby's skull

Below As we grow older, our face bones grow larger, and our appearance gradually changes.

3 years
5 years
10 years
15 years

Bone-building continues throughout our lives. The bone cells are constantly breaking down, rebuilding and reshaping our bones as they are pulled every day by our muscles. And, if we have an accident and break a bone, our bone cells soon repair it.

In later life, our bones grow thinner and more brittle, and our joints begin to stiffen. Regular exercise throughout life strengthens bones, and keeps joints supple.

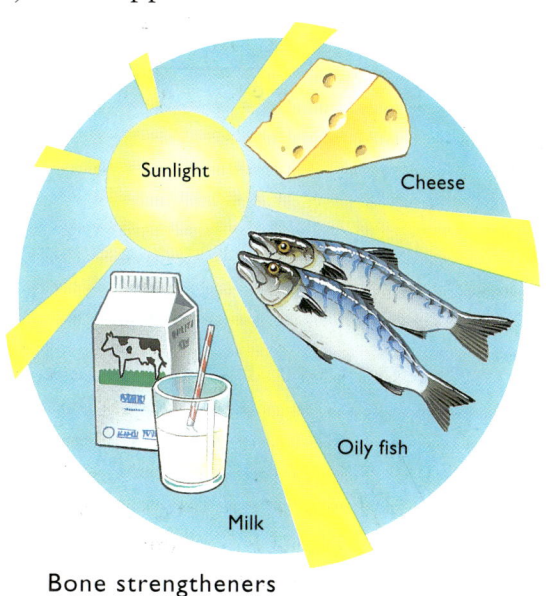

Bone strengtheners

Right Keeping active as we get older can help prevent **osteoporosis**, a disease in which bones become very brittle and fracture easily.

ANIMAL SKULLS

Left A lion's massive jaws and dagger-like teeth help it to kill and eat its prey. Huge cheekbones and a bony ridge on top of its head anchor the muscles that can give such a powerful bite.

Above A dog's long snout houses a very keen sense of smell.

Above A cat's skull has huge eye sockets to hold its large, watchful eyes.

An animal's bony skull protects the brain, houses the senses, and allows its owner to breathe and eat. Every kind of animal has a slightly different skull. This has developed over millions of years to suit its lifestyle and needs. Birds, for example, have feather-light skulls that won't weigh them down in the air. Big cats, such as lions, have heavy skulls with powerful jaws to crush their prey. Plant eaters, such as goats, have a lower jaw that moves from side to side to grind food.

Finding food

Most animals rely on their senses to find the food they need to survive. The structure of a skull often reveals which senses are important for hunting. The huge eye sockets in a monkey's skull show that this animal relies on its eyes to find food. The eye sockets in an anteater's skull are tiny, but the snout is extremely long. Anteaters have poor eyesight, and depend on their sharp sense of smell to sniff out ants' nests on the grasslands.

THE BIG BOOK OF BONES 37

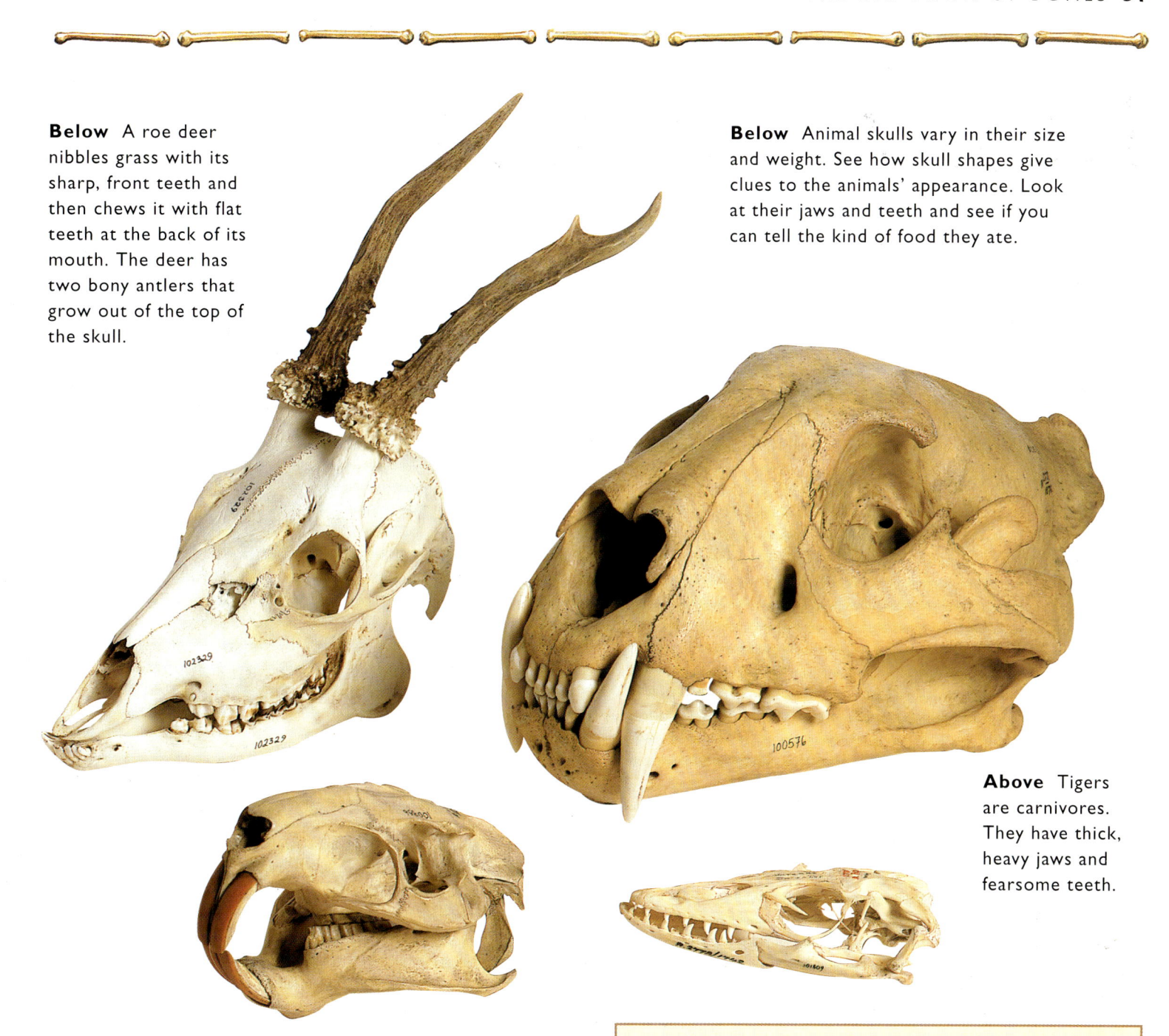

Below A roe deer nibbles grass with its sharp, front teeth and then chews it with flat teeth at the back of its mouth. The deer has two bony antlers that grow out of the top of the skull.

Below Animal skulls vary in their size and weight. See how skull shapes give clues to the animals' appearance. Look at their jaws and teeth and see if you can tell the kind of food they ate.

Above Tigers are carnivores. They have thick, heavy jaws and fearsome teeth.

Above left The coypu is a rodent rather like a beaver. Its four front teeth are long and sharp, and are used for gnawing.

Above right A monitor lizard is a meat-eating reptile. Unlike a mammal, its small, sharp teeth all look the same.

Jaws and teeth

If you want to know the kind of food an animal eats, look closely at its jaws and teeth. Animals with strong, chewing jaws full of broad, flat teeth are vegetarians (**herbivores**) that feed on grasses and leaves. Animals with heavy jaws and sharp, pointed teeth are meat-eaters (**carnivores**) that hunt their food. Animals with medium-sized jaws and different kinds of teeth probably eat a wider diet of fruit, seeds, meat and fish. They are **omnivores**.

BONE UP!

- Hunting animals, such as the cat, have eyes on the front of their head. Their eyes work together, helping them to see clearly and judge distances well.
- Hunted animals, such as the roe deer, have eyes on the sides of their head. This helps them to spot danger all around them.
- An elephant's ivory tusks are really its two front teeth.
- An elephant chews with just four huge teeth. Each one is the size of a brick.
- Male sheep, goats, antelopes and deer have bony horns or antlers on their skull. These are weapons to fight other males.
- Humans aren't the only creatures to use facial expressions. Apes and monkeys do, too.
- A rodent's incisors grow all the time. A rodent has to keep gnawing, in order to wear its incisors away. Otherwise, the teeth would eventually curl round in its skull and stop it from feeding.

Arms, Flippers and Wings

When we look at some animals, such as horses and sheep, it is hard to see any difference between the front legs and the back. But other animals' front limbs evolved to suit their habitat and way of life. With wings, a bird could fly in the air and escape from danger on land. With flippers, a penguin could move through water, and feed on fish in the sea.

A gibbon's arms are longer than its legs – so long, in fact, that on the ground the animal holds them above its head to avoid treading on them. But gibbons spend most of their time in the trees of the rainforest, where their long arms, toes and fingers help them to swing gracefully through the branches.

Below Chimpanzees use their hands to perform intricate tasks. This chimp is using a stick as a tool to dig out some tasty termites to eat.

The human arm

When early humans started walking upright millions of years ago, their arms were no longer needed to support them and help them move. They began to use their hands to develop new skills, such as making tools.

The free-moving shoulder, strong elbow and long arm bones make our arms strong and flexible – able to chop wood, carry loads or gather fruit from a tree. Our hands contain many smaller bones, and this makes them very agile. Think of all the different movements our hands perform as we get dressed or lay the table. Many of the muscles that move the hand bones actually lie in the arm. This keeps our hands small and compact, and able to do very delicate tasks, such as writing or threading a needle.

Above A bird's front limbs are long and light. They are used only for flight.

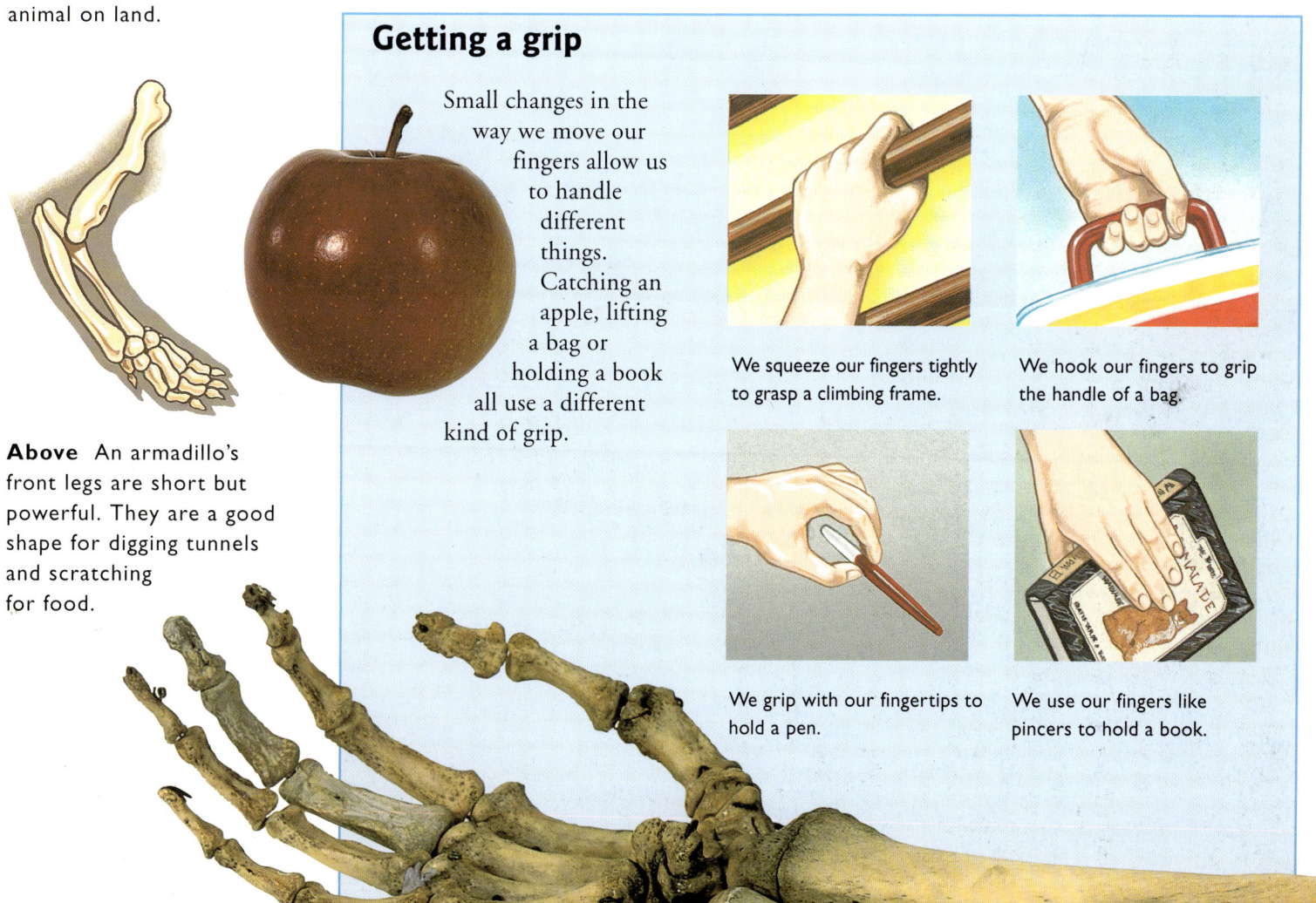

Above A sea lion's flippers power it through the water. The bones are tough enough to prop up the animal on land.

Above An armadillo's front legs are short but powerful. They are a good shape for digging tunnels and scratching for food.

Right A gibbon has long, strong fingers that hook over branches as it moves from tree to tree.

Getting a grip

Small changes in the way we move our fingers allow us to handle different things. Catching an apple, lifting a bag or holding a book all use a different kind of grip.

We squeeze our fingers tightly to grasp a climbing frame.

We hook our fingers to grip the handle of a bag.

We grip with our fingertips to hold a pen.

We use our fingers like pincers to hold a book.

Legs, Feet and Hooves

Every land animal relies on its legs for movement. Legs carry the whole weight of an animal's body so that it can search for food or escape from danger. Some invertebrates, such as millipedes, have dozens of legs; most reptiles and mammals have four legs; birds and humans have only two.

Human legs

The human leg is a well-designed construction kit. The longest, strongest bones in the whole body are found here, and are pulled by big muscles. Our leg bones move at the hip, knee and ankle. These three important joints help us to walk, hop, skip and jump. They also help us to stand upright.

At about the age of one, young children pull themselves up, find their balance and take their first tottering steps. Walking on two legs is rare in mammals, but it is a very useful skill because it frees our arms and hands to do other things.

Even though humans have only two legs, they are long and allow us to run quite fast. Although we may not be as speedy as a cheetah, or able to climb as easily as a monkey, or jump as well as a kangaroo, we can do all of these things fairly well, and a few other things besides!

Above Legs in action! A footballer's strong muscles pull on the bones in his legs, and power his body forwards.

Right A human leg. We balance the weight of our whole body on our long, bony feet. The bones form an arch in the foot, which gives us a spring as we walk.

- The kneecap protects the knee
- The knee joint acts like a door hinge. Stand up, the hinge is open. Squat down, the hinge is closed.
- Larger shinbone carries our weight
- Smaller shinbone
- Bones are thinner and lighter in the middle
- Bones are thicker and stronger at the joints
- Our bumpy ankle is really the end of the shinbones
- The arch of the foot is springy
- Toe bones help us to balance and walk
- Sturdy heel bone

Foot, hoof or claw?

The design of an animal's legs suits the weight of its body and the way that it moves. Huge, heavy animals, such as elephants, have thick, straight leg bones which are as strong as pillars. Some animals, such as antelopes, need to move fast to escape from predators. They bound along, springing into the air on their long, graceful legs.

The shape of the foot also tells us something about an animal's life. The long toes and claws of the sloth help it grip on to tree branches, the sharp talons of an eagle help it to catch and keep hold of its prey, and the light hooves of a zebra help it to gallop away from a deadly attack.

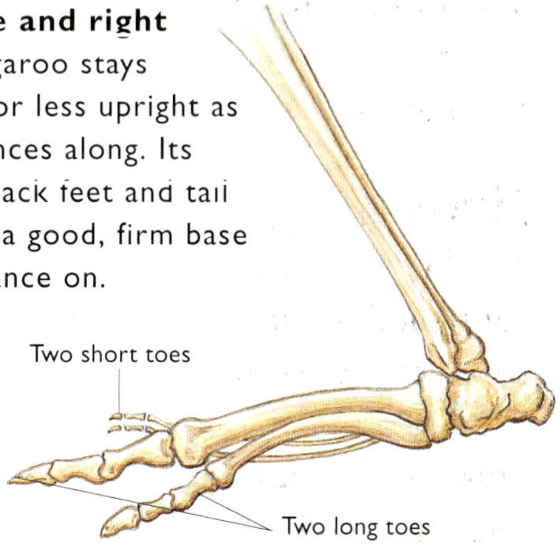

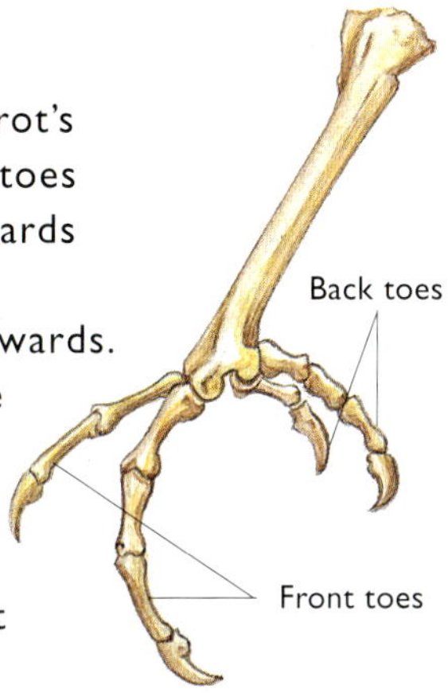

Right A parrot's foot has two toes pointing forwards and two toes pointing backwards. They help the bird to grip hold of things, and to use its feet like hands.

Back toes
Front toes

Above and right
A kangaroo stays more or less upright as it bounces along. Its long, back feet and tail give it a good, firm base to balance on.

Two short toes
Two long toes

Left and right
A horse's hooves are not only light but strong. They take the strain as the horse thunders along.

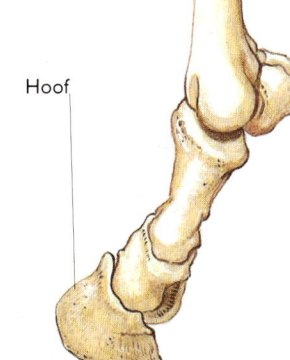

Hoof

BONE UP!

- The fastest land animal is the cheetah. It can sprint at up to 100 km per hour.
- The slowest land animal is the sloth. It moves along at a rate of two metres every minute.
- How long can you balance on one foot? Someone once managed it for over two whole days and nights.
- Birds of prey fly well, but they can only stagger along the ground on their long, curving talons.
- Kangaroos can't walk like us using one foot at a time. They can only hop along on both feet.
- A gorilla's big toe can touch each of the other toes on the same foot. Can you do that?

Bones from the Past

Because bones and shells are hard and strong, they last a very long time. Some of them have survived for many millions of years. **Fossils** formed when the dead body of an animal was buried by sand and mud. Over long ages of time, the mud changed into rock, and the bones were changed into stone.

In some of the Earth's most ancient rocks, scientists have discovered the fossilized bones of long-extinct animals, such as dinosaurs. Sometimes, so many bones are found that scientists are able to reconstruct whole skeletons and put them on display in museums. Like all skeletons, these remains tell us what an animal looked like, how it moved, what it ate and so on. They tell the story of life on Earth.

- The ammonite lived in a whorl-shaped shell 180 million years ago, rather like the nautilus today.
- Fish fossilized well because their skeletons were made of bone. This fish lived about 100 million years ago.
- This shell is known as a devil's toenail.
- Oysters like this fixed themselves to the rocks 120 million years ago.
- Ammonite
- Fossil hunters have to work carefully. They use simple tools to detach fossils from the surrounding rock.

Above Life in the rock: animals with hard shells and bones formed the fossils that we find today.

Right Scientists have reconstructed this skeleton of a dinosaur known as *Triceratops*. In spite of its fierce appearance, *Triceratops* was a plant-eater, and used its sharp horns to scare off hungry attackers.

The human story

Human bones tell stories, too. Skulls discovered in parts of Africa have helped historians and scientists to trace the development of men and women from the early humans of 200,000 years ago, to the modern human beings of today. An old skeleton can give fascinating clues to the past. Worn teeth and damaged or misshapen bones often reveal the person's diet, illnesses and injuries.

Bringing bones to life

1 By working with sculptors, scientists can put 'skin' on the bones of a skull, and reconstruct a human face. Firstly, a cast is made of the skull.

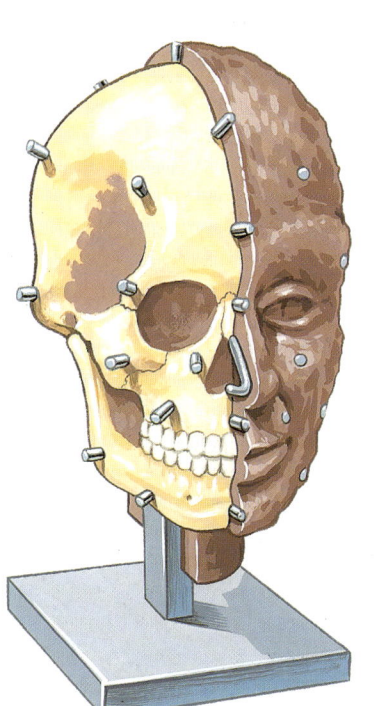

2 Pegs are used to mark the thickness of muscles and tissues that lie over the skull. Clay is used to build up these layers in the correct order.

3 The finished head. The sculptor is only able to guess at the shape of the ears and mouth, but the rest of the features can be surprisingly accurate.

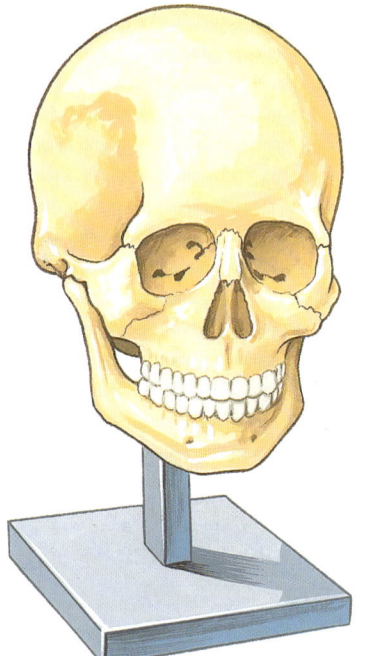

Above Museum experts often help the police to identify human bones. Callipers are used to make measurements that help the scientist to work out the age of the bones.

Bone detectives

Bones sometimes tell stories of violence and death. When the police find human remains, they often turn to scientists for help. By counting, measuring and examining bones and teeth, scientists help detectives to identify the dead. They can judge whether the bones belonged to one or more persons, whether the victims were male or female, what age they were, and sometimes even how they were killed.

Piltdown Man

Bones sometimes deceive. In 1912, a very unusual skull and jawbone were discovered at Piltdown in England. Scientists who studied the bones became very excited. They believed that the human-like skull and the ape-like jaw were many thousands of years old, and belonged to a type of early human. They called him Piltdown Man.

But many years later, the bones were tested, and found to be very much younger. Scientists eventually proved that what had been 'discovered' at Piltdown was a man's skull and the jaw of an orang-utan. It was all a hoax. Some trickster had been playing a joke!

SCARY BONES

Bones have always made people think about death. Because of this, artists often added human skulls and skeletons to their paintings. These symbols of death reminded people that they would not live for ever. Such symbols were especially common in the Middle Ages (AD 500 -1500), when most people died young and whole villages could be wiped out by plague.

Below The Grim Reaper carries an hourglass to remind people that time is passing, and life is short.

A grim reminder

One of the oldest symbols of death is the Grim Reaper. This mysterious skeleton-figure, whose skull is half-hidden by a hooded black cloak, strides through the world, cutting down the living with a scythe. In paintings and drawings, and on statues and gravestones, the Grim Reaper reminded people that life was short, that everyone must die, and that they should be good to each other while they could.

Above Tarot cards appeared in Italy during the 1300s. People used them to try and foretell the future. This card suggested an early death.

Skull and crossbones

Other symbols of death had a very different purpose. The Jolly Roger, the black flag flown by pirate ships, carried a white skull and crossbones. This was a deadly threat. The pirates hoped that its bleak message would terrify sailors on merchant ships, and make them surrender their cargo.

Opposite, below Every November, people in Mexico celebrate the Day of the Dead. They make skeleton decorations, dance in the streets, and remember their dead friends and relatives.

THE BIG BOOK OF BONES 45

Holy bones

But not all bones were frightening. In Europe during the Middle Ages, the bones of holy men and women were honoured and displayed in churches. These holy relics were stored in beautiful containers called reliquaries, which were often made of gold or ivory and decorated with carvings or jewels. The relics were visited by hundreds of pilgrims who prayed for forgiveness, and gave money to the church. The bones brought such wealth to towns that rogues and tricksters soon began digging up bones from burial grounds and selling them as fake holy relics!

Left The bones of holy people were displayed in reliquaries. These precious containers were sometimes made in the shape of a head, arm, hand or foot, depending on the bones inside.

BOOK OF BONES QUIZ

Can you find the right answers to these questions? They are somewhere in the book. You can check whether you are correct at the bottom of this page.

1 *What is an invertebrate?*
a An animal that lives in the sea
b A microscopic animal
c An animal with no backbone

2 *Which of these animals has a skeleton outside its body?*
a An insect
b A shark
c A snake

3 *What is the disadvantage of an exoskeleton?*
a It is too heavy
b It cannot grow
c It is too small

4 *Why do oysters live inside shells?*
a To attract a mate
b To help them to move
c To protect their soft bodies

5 *What is a coral reef made of?*
a The skeletons of millions of sea creatures
b A long line of undersea rocks
c Starfish, sponges and coloured fish

6 *What do all vertebrates have?*
a Wings
b A backbone
c A shell

7 *Tortoises and turtles are unusual because:*
a They move very slowly
b They are reptiles
c They have both an inner and an outer skeleton

8 *How many vertebrae does a snake have?*
a Seven
b Up to 400
c None

9 *Why are a bird's bones so light?*
a They are filled with sponge
b They are hollow
c They are made of horn

10 *Which is the world's heaviest bird?*
a The ostrich
b The eagle
c The albatross

11 *How many bones are there in the human skeleton?*
a About 100
b About 200
c About 400

12 *How much does your skeleton weigh?*
a About half your total weight
b About a quarter of your total weight
c About one-sixth of your total weight

13 *What part of the skeleton protects the lungs?*
a The ribs
b The spine
c The pelvis

14 *A woman's pelvis is wider than a man's because:*
a It contains extra bones
b It gives more room when a baby is born
c Women are fatter than men

15 *Which is the strongest joint in the body?*
a The knee
b The shoulder
c The hip

16 *How long does a broken bone take to mend?*
a Six to eight days
b Six to eight weeks
c Six to eight months

17 *How many bones make up the human skull?*
a One
b Five
c Twenty-two

18 *Which animal has a mouthful of broad, flat teeth?*
a A crocodile
b A goat
c A chimpanzee

19 *How many milk teeth do children have?*
a Thirty-two
b Twenty
c None

20 *Which is the longest bone in your body?*
a Your thighbone
b Your backbone
c Your shinbone

Answers
1 c, 2 a, 3 b, 4 c, 5 a, 6 b, 7 c, 8 b, 9 b, 10 a, 11 b, 12 c, 13 a, 14 b, 15 c, 16 b, 17 c, 18 b, 19 b, 20 a

Glossary

Bivalve A mollusc with two shells that are hinged together.

Carapace The hard, thick shell that protects the body of a tortoise, turtle or crab.

Carnivore An animal that feeds on other animals.

Cell The smallest building block in the body. There are different types of cell (e.g. bone cells, skin cells) and they each do particular jobs.

Chitin The strong but lightweight material that strengthens the exoskeleton of many invertebrates.

Contract When muscles contract, they become shorter and pull on a bone.

Cranium The rounded part of the skull that houses and protects the brain.

Crustacean A group of animals, including lobsters and crabs, that have a hard outer shell and lots of legs.

Endoskeleton An internal skeleton made of cartilage or bone. Vertebrates, such as fish, birds and mammals, have endoskeletons.

Evolve To change and develop slowly.

Exoskeleton A skeleton that forms a rigid covering outside the body. Invertebrates, such as insects, crustaceans and molluscs, have exoskeletons.

Fossil Plant and animal remains from millions of years ago, which have turned into stone.

Fracture A crack or break in a bone.

Habitat The natural home of an animal or plant.

Herbivore Animal that feeds on plants.

Intestines A long tube in which food from the stomach is broken down.

Invertebrate An animal, such as an insect or mollusc, that does not have a backbone.

Ligament A strong band that joins bones and holds them in position.

Mineral A natural substance found in rocks and living organisms, such as calcium phosphate found in bones.

Mollusc A group of animals, such as mussels and snails, that have a soft body often protected by a chalky shell.

Muscles Muscles are elastic-like bundles of fibres, which contract and pull on the bones, causing them to move.

Omnivore An animal that feeds on plants and other animals.

Ossification The gradual change in a skeleton as cartilage is replaced by bone.

Osteoporosis A bone disease caused by a lack of calcium, in which the bones become brittle and more fragile.

Predator An animal that kills and eats others.

Tendon A thick, strong cord that joins a muscle to a bone.

Urine Liquid waste from the body.

Uterus The organ in a woman's body where a baby grows.

Vertebra (plural: vertebrae) One of the small, hollow bones down the centre of the back, which form the backbone.

Vertebrate Any animal that has a backbone. Fish, reptiles, birds and mammals are all vertebrates.

Whorl One of the coils on a spiral shell.

Picture acknowledgements

The artwork is by Peter Geissler (Specs Art) and Bruce Hogarth (David Lewis Agency). Commissioned photography by Kim Sawyer. Other photographs as follows: Allsport 40 (left); Heather Angel 15, 36; David Chapman 35 (top); Bruce Coleman /Jen and Des Bartlett 23 (bottom), /Jane Burton 10, /John Cancalosi 41 (top), /Waina Cheng Ward 11, /Peter Davey 38, /Christer Fredriksson 41 (middle), /Joe McDonald 9, /Fritz Prenzel 41 (bottom), /Kim Taylor 22; Robert Harding 16, 20 (left); Natural History Museum 23 (top), 42; Oxford Scientific Films /Stephen Dalton 4, /Howard Hall 19, /Richard Packwood 5 (middle), /Peter Parks 13 (top); Science Photo Library /British Technical Films 21, /Peter Menzel 25, /Salisbury District Hospital 31, /SPL 34 (top); Tony Stone /David Hiser 45, /John Lamb 6 (left), /Lawrence Monneret 34 (bottom); Zefa 8, 35 (bottom).
Thanks to David Chapman and Mat Rose.

INDEX

Alligator 20
Ankles 24, 28, 40
Anteater 36
Antelope 37, 41
Armadillo 39
Arms 7, 22, 26, 27, 28, 30, 33, 39

Backbone *see also* Spine 9, 10, 18, 20, 21, 23, 24, 25, 26, 28
Bat 25
Beak 22, 23
Birds 6, 22-23, 26, 36, 38, 39, 40, 41
Bone
  broken 32, 33, 35
  marrow 32
  shape 7, 9, 24, 32, 33
  size 7, 9, 24
  structure 32-33

Calcium 32, 34
Cartilage 18, 19, 30, 34
Cat 36
Chameleon 20
Cheetah 9, 40, 41
Chimpanzee 38
Chitin 10, 12
Claws 5, 12, 13, 23, 41
Cliffs 15
Coccyx 25, 29
Collagen 32, 34
Compact bone 32
Coral 16, 17, 18
Coypu 37
Crab 12, 13
Crocodile 20
Crustaceans 12-13, 15, 18

Day of the Dead 44, 45
Deer 37
Dinosaur 42
Dog 36, 37
Dogfish 19

Ears 7, 18, 30, 31
Eating 4, 21, 23, 31, 36, 37, 42
Elbows 9, 22, 26, 28, 39
Elephant 4, 25, 37, 41
Endoskeleton 6, 20
Exercise 8, 9, 32, 35
Exoskeleton 9, 10, 11, 12, 14, 20
Eye sockets 4, 18, 30, 36
Eyes 9, 10, 20, 30, 36, 37

Feet 15, 20, 23, 24, 26, 28, 29, 34, 40, 41
Fighting 12, 37
Fingers 7, 9, 13, 25, 26, 39
Fish 6, 16, 18-19, 26
Flippers 4, 20, 25, 38, 39
Flounder 18

Flying 4, 22, 23, 25, 38, 39
Fontanelles 35
Fossils 42, 43
Fractures 32, 33, 35
Frog 4, 21

Gibbon 38, 39
Goat 36, 37
Gorilla 41
Grasshopper 11
Grim Reaper 44

Habitat 4
Hamster 24
Hands 7, 22, 26, 29, 34, 38, 39, 40, 41
Heels 24, 40
Hips 9, 18, 24, 26, 28, 29, 40
Hooves 40, 41
Horns 25, 37, 42
Horse 38, 41

Insects 9, 10, 11
Invertebrates 10, 18, 40

Jaws 4, 10, 19, 21, 22, 24, 30, 31, 37, 43
Joints 9, 26, 27, 28, 29, 31, 33, 34, 35, 40
Jumping 4, 9, 40

Kangaroo 40, 41
Knees 9, 26, 28, 29, 34, 40

Legs 4, 5, 7, 9, 10, 12, 20, 21, 22, 23, 24, 25, 26, 30, 32, 33, 38, 39, 40, 41
Ligaments 9, 21
Lion 36
Lizard 20, 37
Lobster 12, 13

Mammals 24-25, 26
Mammoth 25, 40
Millipede 40
Mole 5
Molluscs 14, 15, 18, 21
Monkey 24, 36, 37, 40
Moulting 11, 12, 13
Mouse 4
Movement 4, 6, 8-9, 10, 15, 18, 19, 20, 21, 28, 30, 39, 42
Muscles 6, 8, 9, 18, 22, 23, 28, 30, 35, 36, 39, 40

Neck 23
Nose 18, 30
Nostrils 20, 23

Ossification 34
Osteoporosis 35

Pelvis 23, 28, 29, 35
Penguin 38
Perch 18
Piltdown Man 43
Prawn 12

Rabbit 37
Ray 18, 19
Reliquaries 45
Reptiles 6, 20-21, 22, 26, 40
Ribs 7, 21, 27
Running 9, 20, 23, 26, 40

Sea lion 25, 39
Seal 25
Senses 4, 26, 30, 36
Shark 18, 19
Sheep 37, 38
Shells 14-15
Shoulders 9, 18, 27, 28, 29, 39
Shrew 24
Shrimp 12, 13
Skull 4, 7, 9, 18, 21, 23, 24, 25, 26, 27, 30-31, 34, 35, 36, 37, 42, 43, 44
Skull and crossbones 44
Sloth 41
Snake 21
Spider 9, 11
Spinal column 26, 27
Spinal cord 26
Spine *see also* Backbone 5, 18, 24, 25, 26, 27, 29
Sponge 16, 17
Spongy bone 32
Squirrel 5
Sutures 30, 31

Tail 5, 10, 12, 13, 18, 20, 23, 24, 25, 29
Tarot cards 44
Teeth 4, 5, 19, 21, 22, 23, 24, 31, 36, 37, 42
Tendons 8
Terrapin 20
Tiger 37
Toes 4, 13, 20, 23, 24, 27, 34, 41
Tortoise 20
Turtle 20
Tusks 25, 37

Vertebrae 21, 26, 27, 29
Vertebral column 26, 27
Vertebrates 18, 21
Vitamin D 34, 35

Whale 24, 25
Wings 22, 23, 25, 38, 39
Woodlouse 11, 13
Wrist 28

Zebra 41